FOR BUTTER,
WITH WHOM I HOPE TO BREAK BREAD
FOR THE REST OF MY LIFE.

First published 2014 by Voyageur Press, an imprint of Quarto Publishing Group USA Inc., 400 First Avenue North, Suite 400, Minneapolis, MN 55401 USA

© 2014 Quarto Publishing Group USA Inc.
Text © 2014 Tabitha Alterman
Photography © 2014 Tim Nauman

The information in this book is true and complete to the best of our knowledge. All recommendations are made without any guarantee on the part of the author or Publisher, who also disclaims any liability incurred in connection with the use of this data or specific details.

We recognize, further, that some words, model names, and designations mentioned herein are the property of the trademark holder. We use them for identification purposes only. This is not an official publication.

Voyageur Press titles are also available at discounts in bulk quantity for industrial or sales-promotional use. For details write to Special Sales Manager at Quarto Publishing Group USA Inc., 400 First Avenue North, Suite 400, Minneapolis, MN 55401 USA.

To find out more about our books, visit us online at www.voyageurpress.com.

ISBN: 978-0-7603-4598-6

Acquisitions Editor: Elizabeth Noll
Project Manager: Madeleine Vasaly
Art Director: Cindy Samargia Laun
Design: Carol Holtz and Diana Boger
Layout: Diana Boger

Library of Congress Cataloging-in-Publication Data

Alterman, Tabitha, 1979- author.
Whole grain baking made easy : craft delicious, healthful breads, pastries, desserts, and more / Tabitha Alterman.
       pages cm
ISBN 978-0-7603-4598-6 (paperback)
1. Baking. 2. Bread. 3. Desserts. 4. Cooking (Cereals) I. Title.
TX769.A497 2014
641.81'5--dc23
                    2014026053

Printed in China

10 9 8 7 6 5 4 3 2 1

WHOLE GRAIN
BAKING
MADE EASY

CRAFT DELICIOUS, HEALTHFUL BREADS, PASTRIES, DESSERTS, AND MORE

TABITHA ALTERMAN

PHOTOGRAPHY BY TIM NAUMAN

Voyageur
Press

Contents

FOREWORD

William Woys Weaver, PhD
Culinary historian, author, and professor

More than thirty-five years ago, I began planting rare grains at Roughwood, my home and experimental seed garden in Devon, Pennsylvania. At the time, it was almost impossible to find emmer (*farro* in Italian), einkorn, medieval barley like the Celtic *bere* of the Shetland Islands, and a host of other grains that were even then available on a limited basis in natural food stores in Europe. My travels abroad opened my eyes to those extraordinary culinary possibilities, which our homogenized food culture in the United States had marginalized. Furthermore, the rich array of Native American cornmeals has always fascinated me, flavors and textures as different from one another as though milled from different grains altogether. Then there was spelt—recommended for its health benefits by the great medieval herbalist Hildegard of Bingen—which was at one time the basic flour used in pretzel and gingerbread baking.

What happened? Happily, I was not alone with my question. Due to the not-so-green Green Revolution and the rise of GMOs, grain foods have undergone industrial attack, and it has taken a while for those of us who care about the quality of our food to sort it all out in a sensible manner. Counterculture seedsmen (and seedswomen) began growing heirloom grains to feed themselves, sometimes communally; biodynamic agriculture stepped in; and in the 1980s things began to happen. Many books have since been published on whole grains. Now Tabitha

Alterman has introduced her expert voice to this large, ongoing discussion.

I have known Tabitha personally from mutual work at *Mother Earth News* and, most important, her own deep commitment to bringing back whole grains and heirloom varieties into the mainstream diet. Most people who purchase flours from supermarkets do not know what fresh flour tastes like, so accustomed are they to the stale powder that unfortunately seems to last forever and, worse, retains little of its original nutritional value. Tabitha has taken these issues to task and filled her book with all sorts of useful hints and advice on how to get the most from whole-grain foods, how to master the mysteries of sourdough, how to shop for the best values, and, perhaps key to using these foods intelligently, how to store them so they provide the most they have to offer both in terms of flavor and nutritional content.

It goes without saying that *Whole Grain Baking Made Easy* represents a huge amount of creative and time-consuming research, recipe testing, and the saintly patience of Hildegard of Bingen. In short, this book is a gift because between two covers Tabitha has gathered a storehouse of practical information so that you can get down to the important business of reaping the most from your shopping budget and bringing to the table tasteful food with all its inherent nutritional value. Whether you're a novice at baking or an old hand, there are lessons here that will guarantee this book a time-honored place on your kitchen bookshelf.

INTRODUCTION

I wrote this book because the time was right. As an editor at *Mother Earth News* and *Mother Earth Living* magazines, I've been talking to a specialized audience for a while now. Our dear readers are hardcore. They'll grow, make from scratch, or hand-build anything that will enhance the quality of their lives. They're in touch. They live off the land.

Their days are full and rich. Their souls are grounded, present, happy. It has been my privilege to bring useful content about food, cooking, and self-sufficiency to such an inspiring and hardworking group of folks these past ten years. Whenever we publish articles about doing things yourself, our readers actually go and do it. I am, as ever, in awe.

And now, I believe a larger and more mainstream audience has come to the table. Whole grains are popular at last, and more people everywhere are all of a sudden interested in cooking from scratch. Flavorful and nutritious grains are available now that you'd have been hard-pressed to find in a store ten years ago. (Read all about these in the glossary on page 13.)

So maybe you don't need convincing to start baking with whole-grain ingredients or even to make your own flour. If what you seek is a practical guide to getting involved with whole grains, you'll find what you're looking for here. If, however, you're not yet sold on the benefits of whole-grain baking, you can still find the information you need here. I discuss the multiple benefits of whole grains in the pages to come. I'll tell you now, though, that the best reason is flavor: you'll be blown away at the breadth and depth of flavors made possible by throwing white flour over for one of the many better options.

If you're merely whole-grain-curious, and not quite ready to ditch the all-purpose white flour forever, I think you'll still like this cookbook. These recipes are meant to be a jumping-off point. You can choose your own adventures—from, say, 5 percent whole-grain to 100 percent hardcore. Adding just a couple of tablespoons of flavorful grains to a recipe could bring enviable complexity to your home-baked goods. You can even replace one kind of grain with another, to suit your palate. Also, grinding your own grain is practical and rewarding, but it isn't necessary to be able to make *any* of these recipes. I give you plenty of information about how to buy whole-grain flours in Chapter 1. (To gain confidence before adapting recipes, check out page 20.)

Warning: Some of my recipes look *long*. This is because they are designed to help you succeed, to help you take care to choose ingredients carefully, and to do things right at each step along the way. It doesn't mean everything actually takes a long time. I believe it would have been a disservice to you to write recipes that appear to be super simple when all I would've done is omit potentially useful information—especially for novice cooks.

Most of the recipes in this book are actually easy once you get the hang of a few basic conventions. Making baking simpler has everything to do with technique and timing. I'm lucky enough to be able to work from home, so baking fits easily into the rhythm of my day. On page 101, I've detailed several baking schedules that work for different schedules and lifestyles, and Chapter 9 is dedicated to more time-saving tips.

There is one major truth that informs everything I've ever written about food: ingredients matter, and what matters most about them is how they are produced. You will have the most fun and the best luck with the recipes in this book if you choose high-quality, sustainably produced ingredients that are processed in ways that retain their best attributes. My friend Lorene teases me that I write recipes for rich people, but that's really not the case. I give you lots of alternative (potentially pricey) ingredients that you might enjoy, for example almond flour, but I also tell you how you can make many of those ingredients from scratch to save money. If you make a loaf of whole-wheat bread with nothing but flour, yeast, salt, and water, it will taste phenomenally better if you use fresh flour (or grind your own). You don't have to spend a fortune to mix up a good recipe, but you do have to care what you're putting in the bowl.

One of the many unfortunate facts about today's food system is the loss of quality in all arenas, and wheat is no exception. Many of today's grains and, perhaps more importantly, today's common baking processes are inferior to their predecessors. When our ancestors learned to cultivate wheat, they were finally able to give up the exhausting, never-ending search for food. Putting down roots, quite literally, led to stable and sophisticated societies. That civilization has depended on bread as its staff of life for at least six thousand years is good enough reason for me to want to continue the tradition. What I've discovered in mountains of research is that our ancestors were using different grains than most growers are using today. This is why I'm interested in specialized products grown by farmers who plan for better flavor and nutrition, and in many cases are turning back to the nutritious seeds of our past.

This is also why I've spent countless hours investigating baking techniques of the past. By bringing those techniques back into our kitchens, we can reliably hope to craft healthier and tastier foods. You'll read more about these time-honored practices throughout the book—don't skip the Techniques sections.

To learn more about the concepts in this book, visit my website at bourbonandbutter.com.

WHOLE GRAIN BUYER'S GUIDE

In his excellent book *Bread*, Certified Master Baker Jeffrey Hamelman says a baker's goal ought to be "to make breads that are enriching, delicious, and memorable." It's the *memorable* part that has really stuck with me. Ever since I read Hamelman's book, it has been my goal to make memorable food. The best way I've found to achieve this goal is to use exclusively high-quality, whole, real ingredients. When it comes to the flour part, that means I use a variety of fresh— either freshly ground or recently purchased and properly stored—whole-grain flours.

New to cooking with whole grains? A wide world of flavors and textures awaits.

WHY BAKE WITH WHOLE GRAINS?

FLAVOR. Everything in our kitchen starts with flavor. If something tastes great and happens to be good for us, so much the better. In our house, you don't select ingredients on the basis of nutrition alone. That is no way to live.

Whole grains bring the flavor.

Think of white flour from the forever-on-the-counter canister. Imagine dipping in and eating some of that stuff. That's the flavor of white flour. It's almost not there or at least is very faint. Taste a pinch of fresh whole-wheat flour, and it'll be sweet and nutty. Travel further down the road of cereal grasses to amaranth, barley, and beyond, and you'll encounter milkiness, maltiness, even the occasional chocolate note. In most whole grains, these unique flavors are set against a backdrop that is predominantly nutty and sweet—so sweet, in fact, that you can sometimes reduce sugar in a recipe if you use fresh, whole-grain flour.

Some people think whole grains taste earthy and bitter. Often this is because whoever baked what they have tasted was not knowledgeable about whole-grain baking. When real ingredients began to fall out of favor as processed ingredients took over at the turn of the nineteenth century, so did the knowledge of how to buy them, use them, and store them. These things matter. Real flour is perishable. It cannot and should not live in a canister for perpetuity. Real flour is real food. It goes bad. If you unknowingly bake with bad flour, the food you make will taste bad.

Some whole grains do have notes of bitterness or earthiness, but you might actually like these flavors if they are applied properly. Buckwheat, for example, is probably the most assertive of all grains. When paired with bacon and mustard in hearty biscuits (recipe on page 46), you'll love it. In crêpes topped with raspberry Chantilly cream (page 41), it seems surprisingly balanced.

TEXTURE. Yes, that's right. I said texture is a reason *to* use whole grains—rather than a reason to avoid them. For most whole-wheat haters, the biggest obstacle is texture. Unrefined flours are more difficult than refined flours to raise and fill with air.

Some people enjoy dark, dense breads—many Eastern Europeans, for example. If you want breads like that, you can follow Old World baking methods to make incredible rye, barley, and other breads. If you like American-style breads and pastries—in other words, light, light, light— you can avail yourself of different, though equally time-honored, techniques that make lofty breads, flaky pastries, and soft cookies. Without this invaluable knowledge, bakers are misappropriating techniques that work well for white flour. If they could speak, whole grains would be saying, "Treat us differently!"

VARIETY. If you find yourself in a part of the world without a huge array of handmade, healthy foods at your disposal, the easiest way to have them is to make them.

The variety you can bring to baking can be surprising. Even something as simple as using soft wheat for pastries and hard wheat for breads will bring astonishing variety to your baking. Long-time baking expert Shirley O. Corriher was shocked to discover, after years of making artisan breads with her beloved high-protein spring wheat, that she actually preferred the flavor of winter wheat. In her award-winning baking science reference, *Bakewise: The Hows and Whys of Successful Baking*, she writes: "I could not believe how much more flavorful the winter wheat loaves were—an amazing difference in taste."

Think about that. The flavor difference she's talking about results from planting wheat either in spring or in fall. Imagine the flavor differences that can be achieved by employing entirely different species of grains!

Besides keeping things novel, eating a variety of foods rich in different nutrients is plain good sense, nutritionally speaking. As I said before, I don't tend to choose ingredients *only* because they are nutritious, but isn't it nice when you can kill two birds with one stone?

NUTRITION. I have listed nutrition as the last reason you might eat whole grains, because you probably already know this to be a good reason. But here are the facts, just in case. Wheat berries and other grains are plant seeds consisting of three layers: bran, germ, and endosperm. The majority of nutrients are in the bran and germ, yet these are the parts that are removed in making white flour. After the bran and germ are mechanically stripped away, what remains is the starchy endosperm, and it is commonly bleached and treated with up to about thirty chemicals—a necessity when breads must be shipped long distances and remain saleable for a long time. Whole grains are whole because they retain all their parts.

As nutrition researchers gain more knowledge about what makes a diet healthy, one fact is clear: refined grains are bad for our health—and our waistlines. A great body of research shows that these refined grains are responsible for many of our worst health problems.

White bread converts to sugar in our bloodstream almost as quickly as if we were eating pure glucose. When glucose is in our blood, insulin levels spike to help manage it. The glucose is either used immediately or stored as fat, after which our insulin levels dip, signaling us to eat again. If we then eat more refined grains, the roller coaster doesn't stop. Over time, our cells can become resistant to insulin, which leads to a host of ills known collectively as metabolic syndrome. The consequences include everything from high

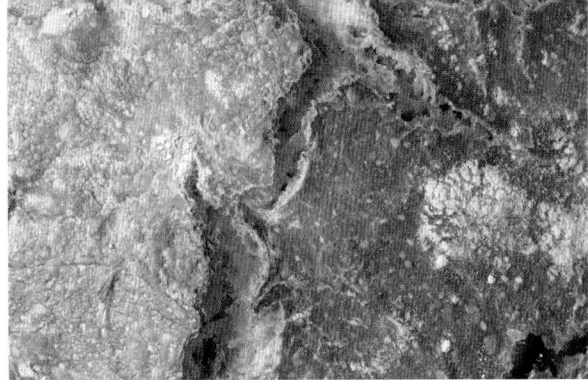

With the right techniques applied to the right flours, you can end up with different textures in whole-grain baked goods.

blood pressure, heart disease, stroke, diabetes, and obesity to asthma, dementia, and cancer.

Unlike the refined white flour in processed food and in most pantries, whole-grain flours contain plenty of fiber, protein, vitamins, and minerals, plus healthy plant compounds such as antioxidants, enzymes, lignans, phenols, and phytoestrogens. These important nutrients can help us maintain a healthy weight, live a longer life, and reduce the risk of numerous illnesses and diseases.

If you get plenty of fiber, maintain an active lifestyle and healthy weight, and eat a wide variety of fruits, vegetables, nuts, and seeds, you should eat whatever kind of bread and pastries you like. In that case, think about choosing whole-grain foods for their wonderful flavors and textures.

WHOLE-GRAIN BAKING SECRETS

HOW TO ELICIT THE BEST FLAVORS AND TEXTURES FROM WHOLE GRAINS

When I first started baking with whole grains, my endeavors were limited to whole-wheat flour. Usually I swapped half whole-wheat for white flour in a recipe. I was treating the whole-grain flour as a stand-in. Now I bake almost exclusively with whole-grain flours, and a much wider variety of grains. I don't expect these to be stand-ins for white flour. Instead, I try to tailor recipes to their individual personalities. I've learned how to get hearty, sour, and assertive results if that's what I want, and airy, creamy, fluffy, sweet, and even spongy results when I want those instead.

The secrets to baking whole-grain breads and pastries with delectable flavors and appealing textures are not new, but because this knowledge is rarely found in today's kitchens, we have to go back in time to discover the best techniques. The various secrets I've gleaned from a mountain of research are sprinkled throughout this book, wherever they are most relevant. I've listed them here mainly to show you that there is a host of knowledge that can improve your whole-grain baking projects. The following are all ways to get the best flavors and textures from whole-grain breads and baked goods, when applied in the appropriate context:

- Choosing, using, and storing grains properly
- Choosing appropriate flours or flour blends, depending on desired outcome
- Paying attention to the unique personalities of different grains
- Whipping cream and eggs before adding them to recipes
- Executing the "creaming method" thoroughly and effectively
- Keeping ingredients cold when "cutting in" butter

- Sifting dry ingredients thoroughly
- Presoaking grains and flours
- Employing pre-ferments, such as sponges and sourdough starters
- Thinking of your sourdough starter as a pet
- Sprouting whole, unmilled grains
- Fermenting bread doughs slowly

- Using especially wet bread doughs
- Kneading bread dough gently, if at all
- Baking bread in a humid environment
- Allowing whole-grain batters to rest
- Choosing high-quality, seasonally available ingredients
- Grinding your own fresh flour at home

Whole grains bring tremendous variety into your arsenal of baking options.

WHOLE GRAINS GLOSSARY

The following whole grains make exceptionally nutritious flours. To reap the biggest dietary benefits, try to incorporate a number of them into your cooking rotation.

AMARANTH

Amaranth is not actually a grain. But it behaves like one and is equally nutritious. Amaranth seeds are especially high in protein, healthy fats, calcium, iron, and other minerals. They also contain the amino acid lysine, which is lacking in most grains. Lysine makes the proteins in amaranth more useful to our bodies.

• *Flavor*: Amaranth has a bold flavor some describe as woody, grassy, or malty. The aroma is noticeably grassy, too. Try using amaranth flour in recipes calling for other bold ingredients, such as chilies, chocolate, coffee, molasses, dark sugars, and pungent spices.

• *Unique Baking Personality*: Amaranth flour can lengthen baking time somewhat and make baked goods dark. When added raw to baked goods, it adds crunch. Amaranth can also be popped in a hot, dry pan. When cooked into a porridge, it gets sticky.

• *Home Milling Notes*: Because amaranth seeds are so small, pour them slowly into your grain mill's hopper while the mill is running, and sift out any seeds that slipped through whole into the flour. Amaranth can also be ground in a grain blender or coffee grinder.

BARLEY

Barley has traditionally been used for making beer and whiskey but also has a history of showing up in breads. It was once the main bread grain in Europe. Barley comes "hulled" (meaning its outer hull has been removed), "hull-less" (meaning that variety doesn't have the outer hull in the first place), and "pearled" (meaning the hull and much of the nutritious bran have been removed).

Of all whole grains, barley has the lowest rating on the glycemic index, meaning it provides perhaps the longest burning energy of any grain. (This is not true of pearled barley.) Barley is also especially high in fiber, protein, and antiaging antioxidants.

• *Flavor*: Barley is creamy, fatty, and nutty with a complex, malty sweetness that has a slightly tart backbone. Barley plays nicely with many sweet and savory ingredients.

Amaranth

Barley

Buckwheat

Corn

Millet

Oats

Quinoa

Rice

Rye

Sorghum

Teff

• *Unique Baking Personality*: Barley has a tenderizing effect on baked goods, which makes it useful in any food you'd like to be soft. Its flavor is mild enough that people probably won't notice if it has replaced some wheat in a recipe.

• *Home Milling Notes*: Barley can be ground in a grain mill or grain blender. Barley can also be flattened into cereal flakes in a roller mill.

BUCKWHEAT

Whole buckwheat behaves like a grain but is actually a seed high in healthy fats, minerals, and vitamins. It has been shown to help control blood pressure. Triangular buckwheat groats are often toasted and sold as kasha, or they are toasted and cracked and sold as buckwheat grits.

• *Flavor*: Buckwheat has a strong flavor you might describe as earthy, savory, or umami. Most people either love it or hate it. Pair buckwheat with other assertive flavors or balance it with strong-flavored sweeteners.

• *Unique Baking Personality:* The unmistakable flavor of buckwheat is definitely best when freshly ground. It can get gummy, so be careful not to overcook it if making it into a porridge. The slow fermentation discussed on page 97 helps mellow buckwheat's flavor in breads.

• *Home Milling Notes*: Buckwheat, raw or toasted, can be ground in a grain mill, grain blender, or coffee grinder.

CORN

Corn classification gets tricky, yet many types of corn are interchangeable. If one is too coarse for your purpose, give it a spin in a food processor before use. **Cornmeal**, made from whole kernels of **dried grain corn** or from **popcorn**, is ground into varying degrees of coarseness, with fine **corn flour** at one end of the spectrum and coarse **polenta** at the other. Sometimes corn is processed with lye into **hominy**. If hominy is finely ground, it's called **masa harina** or masa flour. If hominy is medium-coarse to coarsely ground, it's called **grits**. If it's barely broken or cracked, it's called **samp**.

• *Flavor*: What you're looking for in baking is corn's sweet undertone. The best way to get this desirable flavor—and there are no exceptions—is to grind your own fresh cornmeal—the crème de la crème of homemade grain products. It's worth seeking out heirloom corns that are known to be especially flavorful (see sources on page 156).

Culinary historian and author of *100 Vegetables and Where They Came From* William Woys Weaver favors Delaware Indian Puhwem corn for flour.

• *Unique Baking Personality*: Keep degree of coarseness in mind when using any ground corn in a recipe.

• *Home Milling Notes*: Buy the best-quality dried heirloom grain corn you can find, or use popcorn, which is easier to find. Process to grain mill or blender's finest setting for corn flour and medium or coarse for cornmeal and polenta.

MILLET

Usually used as birdseed in North America, millet is one of the most nutrient-dense foods in Africa, where the seeds are commonly eaten. Millet can be up to 22 percent protein and is also high in fiber, healthy fats, iron, magnesium, manganese, phosphorus, lysine, and vitamins, especially B vitamins.

• *Flavor*: Though flavor depends on the variety, millet typically has a mild, nutty, cornlike flavor.

• *Unique Baking Personality*: Tiny millet seeds can be cooked into softness if they have not been toasted first. If they are toasted in a hot pan first, they retain a good deal of crunch and have a deeper flavor. Millet can add a coarse texture, much like cornmeal, to baked goods.

• *Home Milling Notes*: Millet is best ground in a grain mill or grain blender. You can grind small batches in a coffee grinder, but be sure to sift any whole seeds out of the flour.

OATS

Superfood oats are high in protein (twice that of wheat), healthy fats, antiaging antioxidants, and a type of fiber that sweeps cholesterol out of our bodies and boosts immune function. Whole oats are called **groats**. When chopped (similar to cracked wheat), they're called **steel-cut oats, Irish oats, or Scottish oats**. Most people are familiar with **rolled or "old-fashioned" oats**, which have been pressed into flakes. I avoid using **quick oats**, which are rolled oats that have been further chopped and processed, with the result that they cause more dramatic spikes in blood sugar.

• *Flavor*: Oats are mild and nutty. Often the flavor recedes into the background.

• *Unique Baking Personality*: Oats are moisture-loving, tenderizing, and thickening; they have a chewy, creamy quality that comes through in baked goods. Oats can be used to create various textures. Left whole, rolled oats add chewiness or crunchiness, depending on how long they're cooked. Chop them in a food processor, and you'll have the familiar texture of your grandma's oatmeal cookies. Pulverize them completely, and you'll have moist, fine-textured oat flour.

• *Home Milling Notes*: Rolled oats can be turned into flour in a food processor, coffee grinder, or regular blender. Steel-cut oats and whole groats must be processed in a grain mill or grain blender. Oat flour is best freshly ground. Groats can also be flattened into rolled oats in a roller mill.

QUINOA

Related to amaranth, quinoa is another nongrain acting like a grain. The ancient Incas, who were crazy about this seed, called it the mother grain. Quinoa is a complete protein and is high in calcium, potassium, healthy fats, iron, and vitamins, especially B and E. Its white circles are its nutrient-dense germ. Like amaranth, quinoa is high in lysine, which is absent from most grains.

• *Flavor*: Quinoa is as strongly flavored (and scented) as amaranth, with a good deal of nuttiness and a touch of bitterness. Try it in recipes that will also feature savory ingredients such as nuts, soy sauce, and meat. When paired with sweet ingredients, quinoa's nuttiness becomes more pronounced.

• *Unique Baking Personality*: Quinoa is naturally coated in a bitter substance that can be removed if it's rinsed off before use (rinse in cool water until water runs clear). This should already have been washed off of commercial quinoa flour. There are numerous varieties of quinoa. Quinoa flour can lend an appealing, fatty mouthfeel and heartiness to baked goods. If you want to add something crunchy to a pastry, pop quinoa in a dry pan with steep sides over medium-high heat until most of it has popped and you notice a toasty aroma.

• *Home Milling Notes*: You can grind quinoa, raw or popped, into flour in a food processor, regular or grain blender, coffee grinder, or grain mill. If you have rinsed it to remove the bitter saponins, let it dry before grinding.

RICE

Most of the rice sold in the United States is highly refined white rice that has had much of its nutrition polished off.

Brown rice (and other colored varieties), on the other hand, is whole in the same way wheat can be whole—it still contains its fiber-rich bran and germ. Many people bake with rice flour because it is unlikely to be an allergen.

• *Flavor*: Whole-grain brown rice is nutty and mild, making it versatile. Different varieties have subtle flavor differences.

• *Unique Baking Personality*: Flour made from short-grain sweet rice makes stickier batters and doughs than long-grain rice flours—and thus, fluffier, spongier baked goods. This is a useful property when making baked goods with little or no gluten. The less-starchy flours from long-grain rice behave more like wheat flour, yet with the specific flavors of the type of rice. Rice flour lends a somewhat sandy quality to baked goods.

• *Home Milling Notes*: Rice can be ground into flour in a grain mill or grain blender.

RYE

Rye is most often associated with northern and eastern Europe, where it is the stuff of bread legend. In the grocery store, you'll find light, medium, and dark rye, and pumpernickel, which is whole-grain dark rye. Light rye tastes like a lot of nothing. Medium (and sometimes dark) rye has had some of its flavorful bran removed. If you grind rye berries at home, you'll have whole pumpernickel rye—and you won't be sorry. This delicious grain is in the same category as raw vegetables on some Weight Watchers indexes; that means it's OK as an anytime snack. Rye is high in antioxidants, fiber, iron, and a number of minerals. Rye is able to absorb a ton of water. The extra moisture in rye breads lends to longer keeping quality and an ability to make you feel fuller than other breads do.

• *Flavor*: Rye has a dark, heavy, sweet flavor that is part grassy, part fruity. Many people who think they hate the flavor of rye have never had rye bread made with fresh flour. Many people also think the flavor of caraway seed or sourdough is actually the flavor of rye, since they are so often paired, but rye is sweet on its own.

• *Unique Baking Personality*: Rye needs more moisture than other grains, because it has more bran and fiber to soak it up. If you are swapping rye for other whole-grain flours, be sure to increase the liquid. Adding a little liquid at a time is usually the best method, but be sure to give flour time to absorb moisture so you'll know if it's enough. Because of all

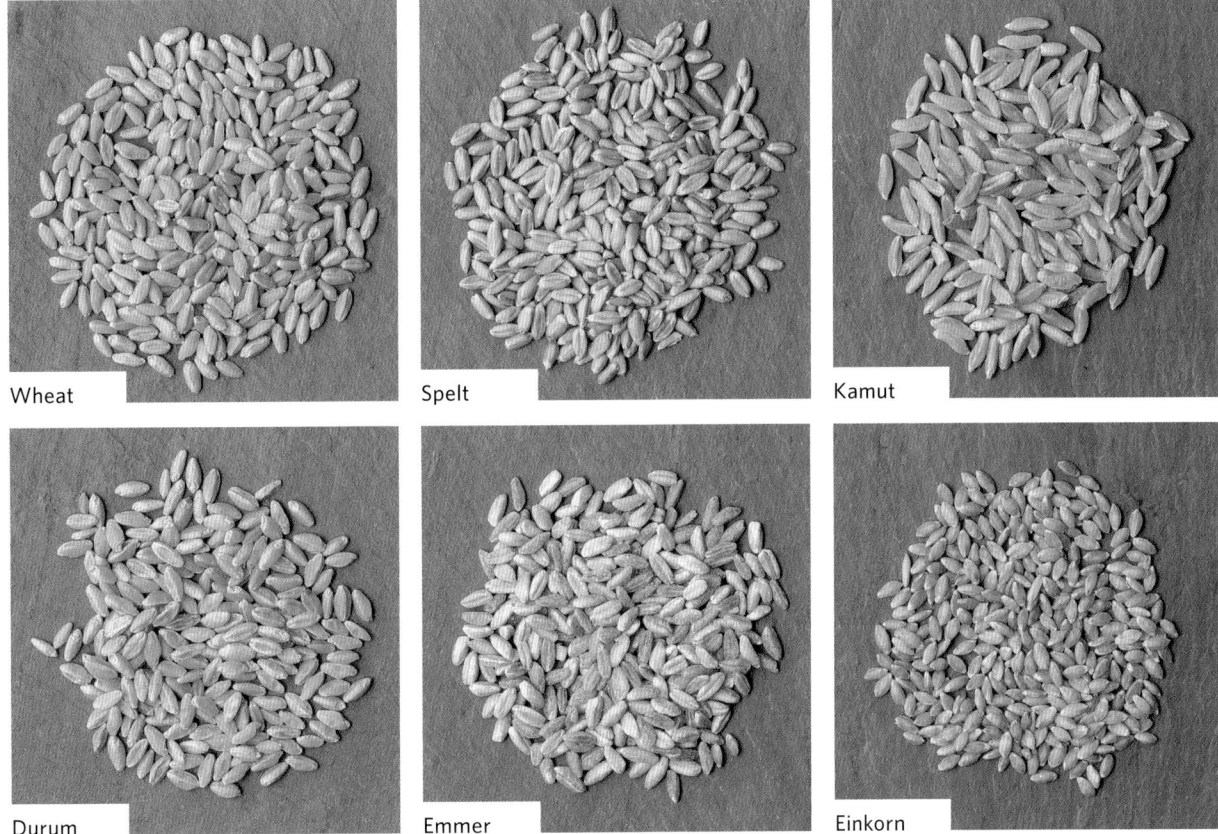

Wheat   Spelt   Kamut

Durum   Emmer   Einkorn

that moisture and the potential for chewiness and gumminess, rye breads are often better the day after baking.

Rye does not like to be overworked, so be careful not to overknead, especially if using a stand mixer. Beware that rye mixtures may be gummier and tackier than if using other flours.

Rye has fast-acting enzymes that quickly convert starches into sugars. This can ruin bread dough if not kept in check. These amylase enzymes are usually balanced with some kind of acid, which could be from a sourdough culture or from an ingredient like buttermilk. Other ways to control the enzymatic action include limiting rising time and using a higher initial baking temperature.

• *Home Milling Notes*: Rye berries should be ground in a grain mill or grain blender. Rye berries can also be flattened into cereal flakes in a roller mill. Rye flakes can be ground into flour in a coffee grinder or food processor.

SORGHUM

Sorghum (also known as milo) is a staple around the world, but most of what is grown in the United States ends up in animal feed, sorghum syrup, or more recently, ethanol production. Sorghum does not need to be hulled, which means when you eat it, you get more nutrients than with other grains. Some varieties are especially high in antioxidants. Sorghum is currently being studied for its potential to reduce cholesterol, lower the risk of cancer, and improve cardiac health.

• *Flavor*: Sorghum flour tastes much like wheat, but a bit sweeter.

• *Unique Baking Personality*: Sorghum can be popped like popcorn, and the flour can be used like wheat in nonbread recipes.

• *Home Milling Notes*: Sorghum can be ground in a grain mill or grain blender.

TEFF

This Ethiopian grass seed is most commonly used to make the sour, spongy bread *injera*, which provides the majority of nutrients in the Ethiopian diet. That doesn't mean your experimentation with teff has to stop there. Teff pairs well with meats, vegetables, fruit, nuts, and chocolate. The tiny seeds are rich in protein and minerals, especially calcium and iron.

• *Flavor*: Teff is strong flavored and malty. Some say chocolaty. It is usually fermented briefly before use, which adds an intense sourness. It obviously works well when soured, but can also be used fresh in sweet recipes, where its rich flavor comes through a bit like molasses.

• *Unique Baking Personality*: Teff has its own yeast strain living on it. If you mix it with water and let it ferment, it will produce a special kind of sourdough batter.

• *Home Milling Notes*: Teff can be ground in a grain mill, grain blender, or coffee grinder. The seeds are so tiny that they can be difficult to grind. When milling your own, pour them very slowly into the hopper with the mill running and sift the flour after grinding.

WHEAT

Like corn, the classification of whole wheat is complicated.

Wheat flour can be classified by protein content: **Whole-wheat flour** most often refers to flour ground from high-protein hard red or hard white wheat, depending on the pigments in the bran layer. Either of these could be spring wheat (planted in spring, harvested in summer) or winter wheat (planted in fall, harvested in spring). High-protein wheat is ideal for breads. Spring wheat has the highest levels. **Whole-wheat pastry flour** refers to a lower-protein wheat, also known as soft wheat. Soft wheat is ideal for pastries.

Whole wheat can also be classified based on how it is processed: **Whole-wheat flour** is ground from the entire wheat berry. **Graham flour** is coarsely ground. **Cracked wheat** refers to wheat that has been chopped, similar to steel-cut oats or rye chops. **Bulgur wheat** refers to wheat berries that have been steamed, dried, and cracked. **Couscous** is made from coarsely ground durum wheat that has been mixed with water, rolled into bits of varying sizes, and dried. **Wheat flakes** have been pressed from whole berries, similar to rolled oats. The most nutritious parts of the wheat berry, **wheat bran** and **wheat germ**, can be mechanically removed from the whole berry (in factories, not so easy to do at home) and sold separately to add texture and nutrients to baked goods. If you are using whole-wheat flour ground at home, you are getting all of the bran and germ already. **Vital wheat gluten** is a processed additive that can be combined with low-gluten bread doughs to increase rise. A tablespoon per loaf is usually sufficient.

Finally, wheat can be sorted by variety:

• **Durum** is an especially hard variety of wheat that is usually ground into coarse **semolina** (after its nutritious bran and germ have been removed), and sometimes into couscous. Its combination of high protein and low gluten is perfect for pasta and pizza. To retain the nutrients of whole durum, you can grind whole berries into a flour much silkier than commercially available semolina or into a medium-coarse texture just like refined semolina.

• **Ancient varieties** of wheat that are the progenitors of modern wheat are becoming more popular for their health benefits, and thus, more widely available. These include **einkorn, emmer,** and **spelt**, which are often confused for one another. This may be because they are so closely related, or because they are all called farro. Be sure you are getting the one you want as there are some differences, though they are all generally more nutritious than common wheat, and for many people, easier to digest. These old varieties also have better disease resistance than other kinds of wheat, which makes them attractive to farmers who don't want to use chemical pesticides—and thus, attractive to conscientious consumers. The reason these may have fallen out of favor over the last hundred years is that they have a hull that is difficult to remove, which makes them more expensive to produce.

• **Kamut**, actually a brand name for organically grown Khorasan wheat, is a more recent type of wheat developed by an organic farming family in Montana. It is related to durum but higher in protein. Its gluten is more tolerable to some people with gluten sensitivity.

• *Flavor*: **Whole wheat** is sweet and nutty, and goes well with a wide range of ingredients from chicken to chocolate. There is often a touch of tannic bitterness, but the bitterness is virtually absent in freshly ground wheat. **Durum** tastes like wheat with a deeper, nuttier character. **Einkorn** has a mild flavor similar to regular wheat. **Emmer** is sweeter and chewier than wheat. For this reason, emmer is one of culinary historian William Woys Weaver's favorite flours to bake with. **Spelt** is nutty, sweet, and milder than regular wheat, with none of its bitterness. **Kamut** is buttery and sweeter than wheat. Spelt and Kamut have become my favorite wheats for baking.

• *Unique Baking Personalities*: For **breads**, use regular whole-wheat flour made from high-protein hard wheat, or try flour made from durum, spelt, and Kamut. For **cakes,** cookies, moist breads, and pastries, use whole-wheat pastry flour made from low-protein soft wheat or try one of the ancient wheats, especially einkorn. For pizza and pasta, durum flour is excellent for its golden color and chewy quality. If you're after a sandy quality, as in graham crackers, go with graham flour.

For its extra nutrition and deeper flavor, einkorn can replace some wheat flour in breads but will not help as much with rise. It needs plenty of time to absorb liquids and can sometimes use a little extra. Emmer has a somewhat coarse texture, even when finely ground. Give spelt batters and doughs plenty of time to absorb moisture and reduce liquid somewhat—add more as needed after it has had a chance to rest. Spelt has the ability to make more gluten than regular wheat, but it is also more fragile. Be careful not to overknead. It's a good idea to combine spelt with regular wheat if your bread will ferment a long time. Kamut has more and stronger gluten than regular wheat. It makes amazingly tall, 100 percent whole-grain breads.

• *Home Milling Notes*: All types of wheat are best ground in a grain mill or grain blender. The softer berries, including emmer, Kamut, spelt, and soft regular wheat, can be ground in small batches in an electric coffee grinder. All types of wheat berries can be cracked or flaked.

OTHER KINDS OF FLOUR

All-purpose flour, bleached or unbleached, is made from a blend of flours to achieve middle-of-the-road protein content. It works adequately, but not necessarily best, for many purposes.

Bread flour, bleached or unbleached, is made from hard wheat high in the kinds of protein that make good yeast breads.

Cake flour is bleached and ground superfine. It has the lowest protein content of all refined wheat flours.

Pastry flour is finely ground from low-protein soft wheat.

Sprouted or malted flour (pictured) is made from grains that have been soaked in water to initiate sprouting, or germination. If you use the little sprouts as-is, they are called sprouted wheat. If you dry them and grind them into a fine powder, they are called "malted" or "sprouted" flour.

If you're new to whole-grain baking, begin flour-swapping experiments with a white-to-whole wheat ratio of about 3 to 1.

Swapping and Mixing Flours

If you are new to whole grains, or if someone in your family is finicky about whole-wheat baked goods, begin your experiments by swapping about a quarter of the white flour called for in a recipe with a whole-grain flour. You can gradually increase the ratio with each successive—and successful!—recipe.

As we've seen, flour comes in many forms and many flavors. You can bake with any combination of flours you like as long as you keep their gluten content in mind. For most yeast bread recipes, your combination of flours must include at least half wheat flour for its gluten content. This is not always necessary in recipes that get their lift from baking powder and baking soda or from specific mixing methods that incorporate a lot of air. Also be mindful that whole-grain flours absorb more liquid than white flour, and they take longer to do so.

FLOURS THAT CONTAIN GLUTEN TO HELP BREADS RISE

Hard spring and winter wheat

Soft wheat

Kamut (wheat)

Spelt (wheat)

Triticale (a cross of wheat and rye)

LOW-GLUTEN FLOURS

Barley

Durum (wheat)

Einkorn (wheat)

Emmer (wheat)

Rye

GLUTEN-FREE FLOURS

Amaranth

Buckwheat

Corn

Millet

Oats

Quinoa

Rice

Sorghum

Teff

GLUTEN-FREE, NONGRAIN FLOURS

You can also make flours for baking from beans, peas, nuts, and seeds. To learn more about making these nongrain flours, Erin Alderson's *Homemade Flour* is a must-read.

BUYING AND STORING WHOLE GRAINS AND FLOURS

WHOLE-GRAIN FLOUR contains all parts of the grain, including oils that eventually become rancid. The best way to ensure freshness if using store-bought flour is to buy as little as you need. Look for an expiration date (you may not find one), or ask a store manager how quickly the product gets replenished. Shop bulk bins at natural foods stores with high turnover. Taste a pinch of flour to see if it's bright and sweet (it should be) or if you detect much bitterness or mustiness. You can also order flour via the Internet.

Though I am clearly a devotee of homemade flour, there are some companies whose whole-grain products I love—and more all the time now that people are getting turned on to real food. In addition to the companies on page 156, check your local farmers market for freshly ground flour.

Store whole-grain flour in airtight containers in the fridge or freezer to prevent the flour from becoming oxidized and the natural oils from going off. It's difficult to give specific guidelines for how long flour stays fresh, but you can generally expect at least a few weeks in the fridge and

several months in the freezer. Some kinds of whole-grain flour, for example whole-wheat, will last a month or so at room temperature. Other grains, in particular buckwheat, corn, and oats, begin to oxidize quickly after being ground. Airtight containers always make the best storage.

UNMILLED WHOLE GRAINS will last indefinitely. Intact grains have reportedly been found in an Egyptian pharaoh's tomb. If you don't have a conveniently located tomb, store your grains in airtight containers away from direct heat and light. Smaller quantities will be fine in a relatively warm kitchen. If you buy large quantities, store them in heavy-duty buckets in your basement or a cool corner of the garage. (Pleasant Hill Grain sells easy-to-use screw-top lids for 2-gallon and 5-gallon buckets.) We keep a shelf on our back porch filled with all kinds of grains and beans stored in the largest size (5.5 quarts) of OXO's BPA-free, snap-top POP line of containers. You can find these at many retailers or through oxo.com. See page 156 for recommended sources of unmilled grains.

Your whole-grain baked goods will always taste best if you use fresh flour. Whole-grain flours can eventually go bad, but unmilled whole grains stay good for years when stored in airtight containers away from high temperatures.

"WHITE" FLOUR

The first record of bread was a flatbread made around 6,700 BC. By 3,000 BC, the Egyptians had learned to leaven it. By the time of the Roman Empire, millers could make a version of white flour, which quickly became popular. That white flour, made by sifting out some of the coarsest pieces of bran, was a distant cousin to today's commercial white flour. I love *that* kind of white flour. I make it all the time at home.

Homemade white flour—which is actually tan—is not to be confused with commercially refined white flour, which contains only about three-quarters of the original wheat that entered the mill, plus some extra junk wheat has never possessed. *What has been removed?* Nutritious bran and germ. *What has been added?* Chlorine, nitrogen oxide, acetone, peroxide, ascorbic acid, and potassium bromate, to name just a few of the chemicals that brighten, moisten, condition, aerate, preserve, sweeten, and, sadly, add flavor.

If you look closely at bran, you'll see jagged edges. In bread dough, these act like tiny razor blades destroying gluten networks, leading to less rise and denser loaves. Instead of leaving most of these inside my breads, I use some of those sifted bits to dust the pizza peel where loaves of bread rise before going into the oven, which means I end up eating the bran on the bottom crust of breads. The crumb remains soft and creamy with plenty of air. Or I find another way to keep the bran in the baked good—for example, sprinkling it into streusel toppings.

YIELD: Scant 1 cup

INGREDIENTS:

Whole-wheat flour (home-ground or store-bought)

INSTRUCTIONS:

① Pour flour through a fine sieve into a bowl. What filters through is homemade "white" flour. What is left behind is nutritious wheat bran.

② Store wheat bran in the refrigerator or freezer or use immediately.

For lighter baked goods, sift out some of the coarsest pieces of bran and use them on the outsides of your baked goods. You'll get all the nutritional benefits of the bran this way, plus some of the textural benefits of lighter white flour.

HOW TO MEASURE FLOUR— YOU NEED TO KNOW THIS

Inexpensive food scales make life easier and cooking more successful.

Instructions similar to this appear in almost every baking book, despite the fact that people ignore them. This concept is crucial, however. The best way to measure flour is by weight rather than volume. Period. A cup of flour can vary by as much as an ounce or two, depending on how it's measured. Measuring cups can also vary by up to about 10 percent in either direction. Weights, as determined by inexpensive food scales, never vary: 125 grams is 125 grams.

Another reason to use a food scale to weigh ingredients is that it will make your life easier. You can put one bowl on the scale and pour ingredients directly into it, one by one, rather than dirtying various prep bowls, measuring cups, and spoons.

A food scale is extra useful when dealing with home-ground flours. If the recipe calls for 20 grams of flour, you can simply put 20 grams of wheat berries into your mill and end up with 20 grams of flour. Contrast that to the following: 1 cup of barley flour is ground from a scant ½ cup of whole barley and 1 cup of medium-coarse cornmeal is ground from ¼ cup plus 2 tablespoons dried corn. Wouldn't it just be easier to measure by weight? Yes. The answer is yes.

Food scales start as low as $20 or so. I've been using my beloved OXO scale ($50) for years, and it happens to be the current favorite as rated by the equipment experts at *Cook's Illustrated* magazine.

STILL PLANNING TO USE MEASURING CUPS?

OK, we can still be friends. Here's how to measure your flour properly. If you have just ground it yourself in a mill, it will be plenty aerated. If you have purchased it in a bag, it will not. Use a fork to fluff it up before measuring. Then reach in with a spoon and scoop out one spoonful at a time into your measuring cup, until the flour is piled up over the top. Now grab a straight edge, like a knife, and scrape the excess flour across the top so that it falls back into your container.

Wouldn't it just be easier to use a scale instead of a fork, spoon, knife, *and* a measuring cup? Yep.

GRAIN MILL BUYER'S GUIDE

Small communities used to operate a mill, where you could buy fresh flour when you needed it. It was grown locally and tasted of a place. It was nutritious and sweet, with little bitterness. Those days are long gone. If you do have a great source of super-fresh whole-grain flour sold at a reasonable price, you may not need to invest in a grain mill. Most of us are not so fortunate.

Lucky for us, making flour in a home mill is easy. If you've already made the leap to grinding your own coffee beans before making each pot of coffee, then making your own flour will seem like a breeze.

The fresher the flour, the better it will taste and the more nutrient-dense it will be.

WHY GRIND YOUR OWN FLOUR?

Here are a few of the great reasons to try your hand at homemade flour:

FLAVOR. Freshness, which can be equated with both flavor and nutrition, is the No. 1 reason to mill flour. The moment after grains become flour is the moment of the flour's maximum potential flavor, after which oxygen goes to work scavenging flavor molecules and degrading fatty acids. Some types of fresh flour, including buckwheat, corn, oats, and rye, are even more susceptible than wheat to fast degradation. This is no different than what happens to coffee beans once they're ground. Many coffee aficionados wouldn't think of brewing coffee with beans ground a week or more ago.

VARIETY. With more than thirty thousand varieties of wheat in existence, you'd think options for nutritious flours would be numerous. Sadly, this is not the case. Research conducted by Dr. Donald R. Davis, a former nutrition scientist at the University of Texas, demonstrates how wheat has declined nutritionally over the last 50 years as farms have become more industrial.

"Beginning about 1960," Davis told me, "modern production methods have gradually increased wheat yields by about threefold. Unfortunately, this famous Green Revolution is accompanied by an almost unknown side effect of decreasing mineral concentrations in wheat. Dilution effects in the range of 20 percent to 50 percent have been documented in modern wheats for magnesium, zinc, copper, iron, selenium, phosphorus, and sulfur, and they probably apply to other minerals as well."

In addition, some of today's varieties have only half as much protein, and there is evidence that old wheat varieties often have substantially higher amounts of valuable phytochemicals.

A few intrepid artisan companies are bucking the trend. Wheat Montana Farms, for example, is one of the few companies where you can buy wheat directly from the farmers who grow it. Their two special varieties, Prairie Gold and Bronze Chief, were selected for superior protein content. At Bluebird Grain Farms in Washington state, the nutritious heirloom wheats einkorn and emmer are grown sustainably and are milled to order or sold whole.

Similarly, Bob's Red Mill, King Arthur Flour, Pleasant Hill Grain, and Urban Homemaker, among others, sell high-quality, whole, unmilled grains for home grinding. If you have a great bakery near you, find out where they buy their flour—many small mills will accommodate special orders. If you notice that a farmers market stand offers fresh flour, ask if you can buy some grains to grind at home. (Find more recommended sources on page 156.)

If you want to bake with a variety of grains beyond wheat, sometimes the easiest way to get these flours is to grind your own. Buckwheat tastes nothing like wheat. This is an advantage, not a disadvantage. I use buckwheat when I want its earthy flavor. I use fresh cornmeal when I want sweet corn flavor. I use oat flour when I want tenderness, and flour made from toasted quinoa when I want extra nuttiness. Variety is the key.

CONTROL. Not only are many of today's flours likely inferior to their predecessors, but they can also be inconsistent from one brand to another. For most bread making, high-protein hard wheat is ideal. Lower-protein soft wheat flours are better for pastries. Maybe you like the taste of white wheat better than red, or perhaps whatever you're baking could use a little extra sweetness from sorghum or a bold accent from teff. By milling your own flour, you have control over all this. You can custom-blend exactly the mix you need, without buying several different bags of flour that you'll then have to find room for in your freezer.

Home milling affords control over texture, too. With a good grain mill you can turn any grain into a fine, medium, or coarse flour to suit your needs.

COST. Whole grains are less expensive than the flours from which they are made. Depending on the price you pay for unmilled grains, you can easily make homemade loaves of bread for less than a buck. However, don't expect to be able to offset the purchase of a mill with grocery savings unless you plan to replace a great deal of store-bought goods with homemade versions.

CONVENIENCE. When did people decide shelf life was the prime virtue? I don't choose ripe tomatoes or fresh fish based on the fact that these items will last forever in my kitchen. Yet we've been trained to think flour should last forever, when it really shouldn't. Unmilled grains, on the other hand, can easily last 20 or 30 years, or possibly forever. Meanwhile, they won't take up prime real estate in your fridge or freezer.

Stand mixer

CHOOSING A GRAIN MILL

There are a few different machines that can make flour. Which one you need depends on how often you'll use it, how easy you want it to be, whether or not you need the machine to perform other tasks, and how much money you're comfortable spending. If you're serious about putting the best food on your table, any of these is a smart investment. Some of these well-made machines may even stick around for your lifetime plus perhaps your children's.

Coffee/spice grinder

Food processor

High-powered blender

MULTIPURPOSE SMALL APPLIANCES

The following appliances serve double- or triple-duty at least. These aren't the ideal grain grinders if you'll be making flour or cornmeal a heckuvalot, but they offer a nice compromise if it's something you'll do occasionally.

Coffee/spice grinder

A coffee grinder is good enough to make flour from some items, such as soft grains, seeds, and flakes. Sift anything ground in a coffee grinder through a fine sieve to remove chunky pieces.

Food processor

If you can grind it in a coffee grinder, you can grind it in a food processor. The blade technology is similar, but the capacity is larger. I've had great success using the KitchenAid 13-cup model. Food processors can be used for an amazing array of other tasks too.

High-powered blender

BlendTec and Vitamix both make powerful blenders that grind an impressive variety of items, even hard grains. Do not assume that another blender can handle this task, unless it has been explicitly rated to do so. A good blender can do many of the same things a food processor does. If you'll use one a lot—for example, to make smoothies, soups, sauces, nut butters, and flour—you won't mind coughing up the $400 or so. The BlendTec machine can grind nearly anything. The Vitamix can too, but it comes with separate pitchers for wet and dry ingredients, making it pricier.

Stand Mixer

KitchenAid makes a grain-grinding attachment to fit their stand mixers. These are good for small batches, but be sure to give the motor time to cool between batches to prevent overheating flour. Stand mixers range in price from $350 to $650, and the grain-grinding attachment is $150, so this is no small investment. Like a food processor, however, a stand mixer has a number of useful applications, and they can last a lifetime. My mother-in-law has had her hard-working KitchenAid since the 1960s.

DEDICATED GRAIN MILLS

There are many types of grain mills on the market, ranging in price from $70 to more than a grand. Google "grain mills" or search for them on Amazon to begin comparing models. Some grain mills are hand-operated, but don't think about getting one unless you seriously believe you will use it. It's possible to enjoy the manual labor, but if you know you're not that kind of person, it'll be a waste of money.

Grain mills are also classified based on how they crush grain: burr or impact plates.

In a **burr mill**, grains are crushed between two plates into various degrees of coarseness. If you've heard of stone-ground flour or cornmeal, it was produced in a burr mill in which the plates were made of real stone. Most burr mills today have composite or metal plates. Real stone mills are prohibitively expensive, plus they require more maintenance over time. They also sometimes have trouble with especially hard items like dry beans or popcorn. Most composite stones can handle these materials. Some mills with metal plates can handle even oily nuts for making nut butter.

Dedicated grain mill

Burr mills grind slightly more slowly than impact mills, usually just enough to prevent an undesirable amount of heat from ruining the nutrients and gluten in your flour.

Durable, well-made, *electric* burr mills include Family Grain Mill ($280), KoMo/Wolfgang ($440 to $600), and Golden Grain Grinder ($600).

High-quality *hand-crank* burr mills include Victoria (formerly called Corona, $70); Back to Basics ($80); Family Grain Mill ($150); Schnitzer Country Mill ($350); Country Living Grain Mill ($430); GrainMaker Grain Mill

Manual grain mills can be inexpensive, but before purchasing one, think about whether you really want to grind flour by hand.

No. 99 ($675) and No. 116 ($1,200); and the wildly popular and well-made Diamant, which has been rated by Lehmans.com as the finest grain mill available today. Many of these are convertible to electric power with separate attachments (not included in these prices), and also offer flywheel attachments to make manual grinding easier.

In an **impact mill**, two interlocking cylinders spin within one another while grains pass through. These don't always make the finest flour. On the other hand, they are inexpensive compared to burr mills. The most popular electric impact mills include K-Tec Kitchen Mill ($180), GrainMaster Wonder Mill ($270), and Nutrimill ($290).

Electric impact-type grain mills make quick work of grinding fresh flour at home.

HOME-GROUND FLOUR IS EASIER THAN YOU THINK

Before milling any grain, make sure it's dry and mold free. Pick out any rocks and pieces of chaff.

If using a **coffee grinder or food processor**, grind small batches. Let the machine cool between batches. Sift flour through a fine sieve to remove any chunks that made it through largely unscathed. If a good deal of the resulting flour is coarse, sift the finer flour out and return the chunky portion to the machine to grind again.

If using a **grain blender** or **stand mixer with grain mill attachment**, follow your machine's instructions to select the appropriate settings.

If using a **dedicated grain mill**, select coarseness and pour grain into the hopper while the machine is running. Or, with a manually operated machine, select coarseness, add grain, and start cranking. Let your mill cool down between batches to prevent overheating flour.

Keep your mill free of flour buildup by following its instructions for cleaning. With my KoMo mill, all I do is occasionally dust it with a stiff, little brush.

Never grind items that your mill is not meant for. Some mills cannot grind oily items, such as corn and soybeans. After grinding oily items in mills that have been made to handle it, it's a good idea to pass a handful of wheat berries through afterward to pick up and remove residual oil.

The grain mill attachment for KitchenAid stand mixers is a logical choice for the would-be flour maker who already enjoys the many benefits of a stand mixer.

QUICK BREADS: GET IN AND GET OUT

Quick breads are so named because, generally speaking, they are quick to make: mix wet ingredients, mix dry ingredients, and stir just until combined. The time investment with these is nothing compared to the waiting game with yeast and sourdough breads, though sometimes you'll need to do a little advance prep, such as chopping or precooking ingredients. Also, because these recipes are 100 percent whole-grain, allowing batters to rest at least 15 minutes before cooking will give grains time to absorb liquids and soften.

Because these breads are less dependent than yeast breads on the strength of gluten, you can experiment with many of the different flavors of whole grains. Check the Whole Grains Glossary on page 13 for ideas.

RYE COCONUT BANANA BREAD

Whenever a banana is about to get overripe, I throw it in the freezer. When I notice a few black bananas have collected there, I make banana bread. If you are only familiar with the flavor of rye in sour recipes, you may be surprised that the fruity flavor of rye works beautifully with bananas, cashews, and coconut.

YIELD: 9-inch loaf

INGREDIENTS:

Cooking spray or lard, for greasing pan

1⅓ c. (104g) whole-wheat flour

⅓ c. (33g) whole-rye flour

⅓ c. (50g) coconut flour (or another finely ground nut)

1 tsp. (5g) baking soda

1 tsp. (4g) salt

About 3 medium-sized, extremely overripe bananas (approximately 1½ c./340g mashed banana)

¾ c. (120g) coconut sugar or brown sugar

2 large eggs (100g), beaten

½ c. (108g) coconut oil or 1 stick unsalted butter, melted and cooled

1 c. (113g) cashew pieces (whole nuts are more expensive and are unnecessary here)

INSTRUCTIONS:

① Preheat oven to 350 degrees Fahrenheit (177 degrees Celsius). Cut a rectangle of parchment paper approximately 9 by 20 inches to line a standard 9-by-5-by-3-inch loaf pan with ends that hang over the long sides. (Later, you will lift the loaf out of the pan by these overhanging handles.) Grease the ends that remain exposed.

② In a food processor or mixing bowl, sift together flours, baking soda, and salt.

③ In a large mixing bowl, using a hand mixer, whisk, or potato masher, mash bananas with sugar until well-combined. Whisk in eggs, then oil or butter.

④ Using a wooden spoon or spatula, fold in flour mixture and cashew pieces just until combined. The batter will not be totally smooth; do not overmix.

⑤ Pour into prepared pan and bake for 40 to 50 minutes, or until a knife inserted into the center comes out clean. If you like to use temperature to assess doneness, the center of the loaf should be about 200 degrees Fahrenheit (93 degrees Celsius). It should still be somewhat moist. Let bread cool in pan for 15 minutes, then cool the rest of the way on a rack. The bread will be even better if you can wait until the next day to slice it, and it'll make excellent toast. Banana bread keeps for several days if wrapped well.

MIX-IT-UP MUFFINS

This is a choose-your-own-adventure recipe. To end up with a signature muffin for your household, follow these basic parameters using your family's favorite flavors.

YIELD: About 24 muffins

INGREDIENTS:

Cooking spray or lard, for greasing muffin tin; or cupcake wrappers

1½ c. (120g) whole-wheat pastry flour

About ½ c. (50g) whole-grain flour of your choosing, or a combination (barley, quinoa, sorghum, teff, etc.; see page 13 for ideas)

1 tbsp. (15g) baking soda

1 tsp. (2g) ground cinnamon

1 tsp. (4g) salt

3 large eggs (150g)

⅔ c. (170g) coconut oil or unsalted butter, melted and cooled

1½ tsp. (6g) pure vanilla extract

½ c. (142g) honey

¼ c. (57g) orange juice (from about 1 medium orange)

3 c. (340g) peeled and grated apples, carrots, pears, and/or zucchini

¼ c. (38g) pumpkin or sunflower seeds

2 tbsp. (6g) freshly grated lemon zest or dried lemon peel

OPTIONAL MIX-INS:

Approximately 1 c. (100g) chopped nuts or flaked coconut

Approximately ½ c. (125g) chopped dried fruit, covered in hot water to soften, then drained

¼ c. (50g) chopped crystallized ginger

Approximately ¼ c. (40g) chia seeds, flaxseeds, hemp hearts, poppy seeds, and/or sesame seeds

OPTIONAL TOPPINGS:

Small handfuls of extra coconut, nuts, seeds, and/or brown sugar

INSTRUCTIONS:

① Preheat oven to 375 degrees Fahrenheit (191 degrees Celsius). Lightly grease tin or line with muffin cups.

② In a food processor or mixing bowl, sift together flours, baking soda, cinnamon, and salt.

③ In a mixing bowl, whisk together eggs, oil, vanilla, honey, and orange juice. Stir in apples, carrots, pears, and/or zucchini, plus pumpkin or sunflower seeds, lemon zest, and up to 2 cups of optional mix-ins.

④ With a spatula, fold in dry ingredients just until combined; do not overmix.

⑤ Fill muffin cups ⅔ full. This is easiest to do with a 3-ounce, spring-loaded ice cream or cookie scoop. If desired, sprinkle on selected toppings.

⑥ Bake 18 to 22 minutes or until a toothpick inserted into the center comes out clean or the internal temperature registers 200 degrees Fahrenheit (93 degrees Celsius). Muffins should be somewhat moist. Allow them to cool in the pan set on a rack for 5 minutes before popping them out to finish cooling completely. If wrapped tightly, muffins will keep for several days.

SHRIMP-AND-GRIT MUFFINS

These muffins bring all the flavors of old-fashioned shrimp 'n' grits into individual hand-held treats. This recipe takes the longest of all the so-called quick breads in this chapter, because there is significant advance prep. But, hey, they freeze well for a few months, so make extras while you're at it. For the best corn flavor, use freshly ground corn.

YIELD: 24 muffins

INGREDIENTS:

1 c. (175g) coarsely ground cornmeal or polenta

1 c. (227g) rapidly boiling water

1 c. (227g) buttermilk, kefir, or yogurt

2 tbsp. (29g) honey (optional, but brightens corn flavor)

2 large eggs (100g)

6 scallions

10 oz. (280g) bacon (about 8 thick-cut strips)

1 lb. (454g) shrimp, peeled, de-veined, and chopped into bite-sized pieces

1 to 2 jalapeños, depending on desired heat, diced

3 cloves garlic, minced

1 tbsp. (7g) Cajun seasoning

1 c. (96g) corn flour

1 tsp. (4g) salt

Several twists and then several more twists of freshly ground black pepper

2 tsp. (8g) baking powder

¾ tsp. (4g) baking soda

8 oz. (227g) Cheddar cheese, grated with grater's largest hole

Hot sauce, such as Tabasco or Crystal, for serving

INSTRUCTIONS:

① Put cornmeal in large work bowl. Bring water to rapid boil and pour immediately over cornmeal while whisking. Hot water helps gelatinize starches in corn and form a "corn mush." The mush should be soft enough to be able to stir in more ingredients without much trouble. If it's not, add more hot water, a little at a time.

② Whisk in buttermilk and honey, then eggs. Set aside.

③ Preheat oven to 425 degrees Fahrenheit (218 degrees Celsius).

④ Finely chop scallions, separating dark green parts from white and pale green parts. Stir dark green scallions into corn mush.

⑤ Cook bacon on medium-high heat. When slightly crispy, transfer to towels to drain.

⑥ Reduce heat to medium. To hot bacon grease, add shrimp, jalapeño, garlic, white and pale green parts of scallions, and Cajun seasoning. Sauté a few minutes, until shrimp are cooked through. Scrape contents of sauté pan into a work bowl. Chop bacon into bite-sized pieces, and stir it into shrimp mixture. Set aside.

⑦ Before washing your sauté pan, sop up bacon grease with a paper towel, and use the towel to grease your muffin pan.

⑧ In another work bowl (you'll have three going at this point—my apologies), stir together corn flour, baking powder, baking soda, salt, and pepper.

⑨ Pour corn mush over flour mixture, then dump in shrimp mixture and cheese. Gently fold batter together with spatula, until just combined. The batter should be thick but pourable. If it's dry or stiff, add just enough buttermilk to reach pourable consistency.

⑩ Scoop batter into greased muffin pan, filling cups to nearly full. This is easiest with a 3-ounce, spring-loaded ice cream scoop (also known as a disher or cookie scoop). Bake for 15 to 20 minutes, or until muffin tops are crackly and golden brown and bits of cheese on top are dark and crispy. A knife inserted into a muffin should come out clean. Transfer pan to cooling rack for 5 minutes before popping them out. Serve with hot sauce.

SIMPLE SKILLET CORNBREAD

Though many cornbreads contain sugar, this one does not. That's because you'll be using high-quality whole-grain cornmeal (ideally freshly ground), which is naturally a little bit sweet. (See recommended sources on page 156). If extra sweetness is desired, serve wedges with the Cinnamon Honey Butter on page 40 or the Maple Butter on page 130. Cornbread is also delicious smeared with blackberry or raspberry preserves.

If you prefer a cakier cornbread, replace ½ cup (175 grams) cornmeal with ½ cup (40 grams) whole-wheat pastry flour.

YIELD: One 8- or 9-inch pan (about 8 servings)

INGREDIENTS:

2½ c. (438g) coarse, whole-grain cornmeal or polenta

1¼ c. (284g) milk (preferably whole)

2 large eggs (100g)

6 tbsp. (81g) bacon grease, lard (preferably from pastured pigs), or unsalted butter, at room temperature

2 tsp. (10g) baking powder

1 tsp. (4g) salt

INSTRUCTIONS:

① Preheat oven to 450 degrees Fahrenheit (232 degrees Celsius). Place your 8- or 9-inch cast-iron skillet in the oven during preheat. (You can also use a traditional cornstick pan. Cornsticks bake faster, usually in about 15 minutes.)

② Soak cornmeal in milk for 20 minutes.

③ Beat eggs in a small bowl, then beat 4 tablespoons of grease into eggs until well-mixed. Whisk egg-oil mixture into soaked cornmeal, then sprinkle baking powder and salt evenly over batter and whisk to combine well.

④ With a hot pad, remove hot pan from oven and set on stovetop. Carefully add remaining 2 tablespoons grease to skillet, then pour in batter. Adding batter to a hot pan creates a crackling crust and gives the bread a quick lift.

⑤ Bake 20 to 25 minutes, until top is golden and a toothpick inserted into center comes out clean, or until internal temperature registers 190 degrees Fahrenheit (88 degrees Celsius).

⑥ Cut wedges and serve directly from pan. Wrap leftovers tightly and they'll keep for several days.

MULTIGRAIN WAFFLES with EASY FRUIT SAUCE

These waffles happen at least monthly in our house, but they're different every time. We use whatever nuts and flours are left in the freezer from a previous recipe and whatever fruits are in season and on hand. They make great pancakes too.

YIELD: 6 to 8 waffles

INGREDIENTS:

1 c. (125g) whole-wheat flour

Approximately ½ c. (50g) whole-grain or nut flour of your choosing, or a mixture

1 tsp. (4g) salt

1½ tsp. (10g) baking powder

1 large egg (50g)

1½ c. (340g) whole milk (or almond or coconut milk), at room temperature

1 tsp. (4g) vanilla

2 tbsp. (28g) orange juice

2 tbsp. (28g) honey (optional)

¼ c. (57g) butter or coconut oil, melted and cooled slightly

¼ c. (20g) whole, rolled oats, wheat flakes, or rye flakes

1 to 2 tbsp. (9 to 18g) flaxseed, chia seeds, hemp seeds, or a mixture

Cooking spray or grease for waffle iron

INSTRUCTIONS:

① Whisk flours, salt, and baking powder together in a mixing bowl or food processor. Add wet ingredients and process or whisk just until combined, scraping down bowl with spatula as necessary.

② Pour batter into a mixing bowl (preferably one with a lid) and gently fold oats and seeds into batter. Cover and let stand a minimum of 45 minutes, or preferably overnight in the refrigerator.

③ About 10 minutes before making waffles, preheat waffle iron and set oven or toaster oven to warm setting.

④ When waffle iron is hot, grease it with a pastry brush or with cooking spray. Pour about ⅓ cup batter into middle and press the top of the iron down completely. When you see steam coming out of the iron, try to lift the top of the iron gently. If it doesn't lift easily, keep cooking. When the top lifts easily and the waffle is as crispy as you'd like (I like super-crispy waffles), pluck it out with a fork. Keep waffles warm in oven or toaster oven. Serve with Easy Fruit Sauce (below). You might also like some of the Cinnamon Honey Butter on page 40 or the Maple Butter on page 130.

EASY FRUIT SAUCE

This pancake and waffle topping is truly easy. Dump whatever fruit and sweetener you've got into a saucepan, plus a pinch of cornstarch if you happen to have some. Plan on about a handful of fruit and a teaspoon of sweetener per person. Set it on the back burner over medium-low heat while you work on the waffles. Stir occasionally. Add a little bit of water whenever it gets too thick. My favorite version of this sauce is raspberries with agave nectar.

CORNMEAL PANCAKES WITH CINNAMON HONEY BUTTER

For the best pancakes, grind your own cornmeal or use the freshest real, whole-grain cornmeal you can find. These pancakes omit the traditional egg and flour, and you can really taste the corn. If you prefer a less grainy texture, mix in 1 large egg (50 grams) and ¼ cup (20 grams) whole-wheat pastry flour in Step 3. Because you will have added whole-grain flour, let batter rest half an hour before using.

YIELD: 6 to 8 servings

INGREDIENTS:

2 c. (248g) medium-coarse, whole-grain cornmeal

2 c. (454g) water

½ to 1 c. (113g to 227g) whole milk

1½ tsp. (6g) salt

Tiny pinch stevia or pinch brown sugar (optional; brightens corn flavor)

½ c. (108g) bacon grease, lard, melted butter, or oil

INSTRUCTIONS:

① The night before making pancakes, bring cornmeal and water to a boil, then remove from heat. Allow mixture to cool to room temperature, then cover and refrigerate for use in the morning.

② Preheat oven or toaster oven to warm setting.

③ Stir milk, salt, and optional sweetener into cornmeal mixture, adding more or less milk as needed to make a thick but pourable batter. Stir in half the grease.

④ Heat a skillet or griddle over medium-high heat. When pan is hot, add a thin layer of grease. Pour out individual pancakes. Flip them when you see bubbles on top. Cook until golden brown on both sides.

⑤ Transfer cooked pancakes to oven or toaster oven to keep warm until serving. Serve with Cinnamon Honey Butter (recipe below).

CINNAMON HONEY BUTTER

Most honey butter recipes have a 1:1 honey-to-butter ratio, but I find this lower-sugar compound butter to be sweet enough even to skip pouring syrup on my pancakes.

YIELD: About 1 cup (258 grams) compound butter

INGREDIENTS:

2 sticks (227g) butter, at room temperature

2 tbsp. (29g) honey

1 tsp. (2g) ground cinnamon

INSTRUCTIONS:

① Using a hand mixer or stand mixer fitted with paddle attachment, beat butter, honey, and cinnamon on medium speed until fluffy, a few minutes.

② Remove to a bowl for immediate use. Or shape into a log, wrap in wax paper, and refrigerate to firm up so you can cut out perfect pats later.

BUCKWHEAT CRÊPES
WITH RASPBERRY CHANTILLY CREAM

Buckwheat is a classic flour for crêpe-making. It imparts an unmistakably earthy flavor and a lovely texture. You'll find buckwheat crêpes, or *galettes*, at nearly all the crêperies in Paris, where they are usually combined with savory ingredients. Here we take them in a lightly sweet direction and add a bit of hooch.

Because crêpes do not need to rise, if you like, you may use all buckwheat flour instead of part wheat and part buckwheat.

You can make this batter the night before you plan to make crêpes, but for the lightest crêpes, allow it to come to room temperature before cooking.

YIELD: About 8 crêpes

INGREDIENTS:

½ c. (40g) whole-wheat pastry flour

¼ c. (26g) buckwheat flour

¼ tsp. (1g) salt

1 tbsp. (18g) honey

1 tsp. (4g) vanilla extract

⅔ c. (170g) whole milk

2 large eggs (100g)

1 tbsp. (14g) unsalted butter, melted

1 tbsp. (14g) orange juice

Unsalted butter, for crêpe pan

1 batch Raspberry Chantilly Cream (next page)

1½ c. (227g) raspberries

INSTRUCTIONS:

① Preheat oven or toaster oven to warm setting.

② Whisk flours and salt together in a mixing bowl or food processor. Add wet ingredients and process or whisk until combined, scraping down bowl with spatula as necessary. Let batter rest at least 15 minutes.

③ Heat crêpe pan or griddle over medium-high heat and grease with butter. Ladle about ¼ cup of batter onto pan, tilting pan to coat surface. Cook for about a minute. Use a spatula to lift the edge and check for golden spots. Flip and cook second side for 1 minute. Slide onto a pan and transfer it to oven or toaster oven to keep crêpes warm. Serve with Raspberry Chantilly Cream (next page) and fresh raspberries.

RASPBERRY CHANTILLY CREAM

This whipped cream is easy to make to accompany a number of desserts. Vary the flavor with different spirits, such as coffee or hazelnut liqueur.

YIELD: About 1¼ cup (274 grams)

INGREDIENTS:

1 c. (227g) cream

1 tsp. (4g) vanilla extract

Pinch salt

1 oz. (28g) Chambord (black raspberry liqueur)

2 tbsp. (15g) powdered sugar, optional

INSTRUCTIONS:

In a mixing bowl with a hand mixer (or a whisk if your muscles are up for it), beat cream, vanilla, salt, and liqueur until soft peaks form. Cover and refrigerate until serving time.

Make Your Own

FAST-ACTING BAKING POWDER

Precombined baking powder can lose its power over time, yet its individual components last indefinitely. Keep alkaline baking soda and acidic cream of tartar in the pantry and you can make fresh baking powder on demand.

Note that this baking powder will act faster than store-bought double-acting baking powder, because nearly three-quarters of the carbon dioxide it produces will be released in the first couple of minutes after it is hydrated.

Some people prefer the flavor of homemade baking powder because it does not contain the additional fillers that commercial products contain. That's also why this recipe that makes three-fourths of a teaspoon of baking powder can be used to replace each full teaspoon called for in a recipe.

YIELD: Enough baking powder to replace 1 teaspoon of baking powder in recipes

INGREDIENTS:

¼ tsp. (1g) baking soda

½ tsp. (2g) cream of tartar

INSTRUCTIONS:

Sift ingredients together. Store extras in an airtight container for up to a month.

Technique

HOW TO SIFT—AND WHY YOU SHOULD

Baked goods get their lift initially from bubbles formed during mixing. In yeast breads, those bubbles are expanded by the carbon dioxide gas that yeast cells release. Because yeast cells take a long time to do this, bread doughs must have a gluten network strong enough to hold bubbles for a long time.

Wet-batter quick breads, such as banana bread and corn muffins, on the other hand, don't need the strength of gluten because their bubbles are expanded by the faster reactions of chemical leaveners. Just like carbon dioxide from yeast cells, the carbon dioxide from baking soda and baking powder expand bubbles in batter. Finally, during baking, steam from liquids in the dough or batter cause the bubbles to expand even more.

Food processors sift dry ingredients incredibly well—a key to even distribution.

Sifting dry ingredients well ensures that leaveners will be distributed evenly throughout a batter—essential for good rise. Old-school flour sifters that you crank or shake to get flour to pass through sieves work just as well today as they always have. My favorite method for sifting flour, however, is to process it in a food processor with whatever other dry ingredients are in a recipe, including baking powder and baking soda. It only takes about 5 seconds, and with the food processor method, you get the added benefit of superfine flour.

When all you've put in the machine are dry ingredients, it's easy to clean by simply rinsing or shaking it out. I love my KitchenAid 13-cup food processor for this and numerous other tasks. (You can also use a hand mixer or whisk to thoroughly mix and distribute dry ingredients, but those methods won't make flour finer.)

Chapter 4

BISCUITS, SCONES, AND PIES:
UNITED IN BUTTERY GOODNESS

Most people agree the best biscuits, scones, and pies are both tender and flaky. The secret to creating pastry like this is engineering numerous layers that flake apart from each other. With pie crusts, you want these layers relatively compact; whereas a biscuit (or scone) is basically pie dough that has been lifted with carbon dioxide produced by a chemical leavener, usually baking powder.

Memorable biscuits and pies usually also taste buttery. You can make them with many different fats, but you should include at least some butter if you want that flavor. My favorite method combines equal parts butter and lard for a great balance of texture and flavor. It's worth seeking out butter made from cultured cream that has a high fat percentage (more than 80 percent) and nutritious pastured lard that comes from sustainably managed farms. Leaf lard is the highest quality for baking, with the least porky flavor.

Many biscuits and pies taste buttery, but the white flour in their recipes contributes little flavor of its own. The recipes here provide the tasty—and more healthful—backbone that comes from nutty whole grains.

BACON BUCKWHEAT BISCUITS
with SPICY HONEY MUSTARD GLAZE

Buckwheat has a strong flavor, but here it is balanced by the equally strong flavors of smoky bacon and honey mustard. You may substitute another whole-grain flour for the buckwheat portion.

YIELD: 8 to 10 biscuits

INGREDIENTS:

8 thick-cut strips (280g) bacon

2⅔ c. (214g) whole-wheat pastry flour

⅔ c. (70g) buckwheat flour

1 tbsp. plus ½ tsp. (17g) baking powder

1 tsp. (5g) baking soda

1 tsp. (4g) salt

1 tsp. (2g) cinnamon

1 stick (8 tbsp./113g) unsalted butter, cut into small pats or grated, and kept cold (ideally in freezer)

1 large egg (50g)

1½ c. (56g) buttermilk, kefir, or yogurt

INSTRUCTIONS:

① Line baking sheet with parchment paper or silicone mat, or grease lightly with cooking spray. Place pan in freezer or refrigerator until use.

② Fry bacon until cooked through but tender. Drain and roughly chop. Set aside.

③ In a food processor or mixing bowl, sift together flours, baking powder, baking soda, salt, and cinnamon. Using your fingertips, two forks, a pastry blender, or the careful pulsing action of a food processor, rub or cut in butter. The smallest pieces should be no larger than a pea, and roughly half the flour should be coated in fat. Put bowl in freezer or refrigerator while you mix the wet ingredients.

④ In a mixing bowl, beat egg into buttermilk. With a large spatula, fold chilled, dry ingredients and bacon into wet ingredients, just until combined. Now is a good time to preheat oven to 450 degrees Fahrenheit (232 degrees Celsius).

Put a large piece of parchment or wax paper on counter. Dump dough onto it. Holding onto dough from the outsides of the paper, fold dough over onto itself a few times, attempting to form a 1-inch-thick rectangle. Remove chilled baking sheet from freezer. Cut biscuits out of dough and place them on baking sheet an inch apart. Biscuit cutters come in all sizes. I like 1½-, 2-, or 2½-inch biscuits. When cutting biscuits, try to keep the sides from crimping together to ensure they puff up and rise well. To do this, push a sharp biscuit cutter straight down, then twist.

⑤ Bake 15 to 17 minutes. Serve warm, drizzled with honey mustard glaze (right).

SPICY HONEY MUSTARD GLAZE

Use this glaze to balance the strong flavor of buckwheat. It's also yummy on roasted meats.

INGREDIENTS:

2 tbsp. (28g) water

½ stick (4 tbsp./57g) unsalted butter, cut into small pieces

½ c. (142g) honey

½ tsp. (2g) salt (unless your butter is salted)

1 tsp. (2g) chili powder

2 tbsp. (18g) dry mustard powder, such as Coleman's

INSTRUCTIONS:

Bring water to boil. Whisk in butter one piece at a time. Whisk in honey, salt, chili powder, and mustard powder until combined. Keep warm until use.

Recipe by Tim Nauman

PUMPKIN WALNUT DROP BISCUITS

Pumpkin adds flavor, moisture, nutrition, and color to basic drop biscuits. (Find purée instructions on next page.) If the pumpkin is especially sweet, omit brown sugar.

YIELD: About 14 biscuits

INGREDIENTS:

1 c. (100g) walnut halves or pieces (my favorite are sweet English walnuts)

1½ c. (120g) whole-wheat pastry flour

1½ tsp. (8g) baking powder

¼ tsp. (1g) baking soda

1 tsp. (4g) salt

2 tbsp. (238g) brown sugar (optional)

1 stick (8 tbsp./113g) unsalted butter, cut into small pats or grated, and kept cold (ideally in freezer)

½ c. (135g) pumpkin purée (page 49)

1 c. (227g) buttermilk, kefir, or yogurt

Honey, for drizzling over warm biscuits (optional)

INSTRUCTIONS:

① Line baking sheet with parchment paper or silicone mat, or grease lightly with cooking spray. Chill pan in freezer or refrigerator until use.

② In a food processor or mixing bowl, sift together flour, baking powder, baking soda, salt, and sugar.

③ Add walnuts and pulse a couple of times. Mixture will be chunky.

④ Using your fingertips, two forks, a pastry blender, or the careful pulsing action of a food processor, rub or cut in butter. The smallest pieces should be no larger than a pea, and roughly half the flour should be coated in fat. Chill bowl in freezer or refrigerator while you mix wet ingredients.

⑤ In a mixing bowl, stir together pumpkin purée and buttermilk until well mixed.

⑥ With a large spatula, fold chilled, dry ingredients into wet ingredients, just until combined. This is a good time to preheat oven to 450 degrees Fahrenheit (232 degrees Celsius).

⑦ Lightly grease a ¼-cup measuring cup or spring-loaded cookie scoop. Use it to scoop biscuit dough onto chilled baking sheet, re-greasing as needed. Leave an inch between biscuits. Chill again for at least 15 minutes. Bake 15 to 17 minutes, or until tops are deep golden brown. Serve warm, with honey if desired.

FREEZER BISCUITS AND SCONES

To make biscuits and scones in advance to have ready whenever you want one, follow recipe through the point that dough is placed on baking sheet. Cover pan with plastic wrap and freeze overnight. In the morning, pop firm, frozen biscuits and scones into freezer container labeled with cooking time and temperature. When it's time to bake them, don't worry about thawing. Just thaw as long as it takes oven to preheat, and add a few minutes to baking time.

PUMPKIN PURÉE

When pumpkins and winter squash are in season, I try to make plenty of purée to store in the freezer, because it's so easy to make and so superior to canned purée. Be sure to choose a pie pumpkin rather than a carving pumpkin. Smaller pie pumpkins are generally sweetest.

According to Amy Goldman, author of *The Compleat Squash*, the *Cucurbita pepo* variety known as 'Winter Luxury Pie' makes a smooth and velvety pumpkin pie custard. "When cut into a wedge on a plate, it holds its shape, color, and flavor long after the competition has keeled over and died," she says. 'Kumi Kumi' is another of her favorite varieties, but there are many great pumpkins and squash to choose from.

INGREDIENTS:

1 whole pie pumpkin (a 2½-lb. pumpkin yields about 2 c. of purée, or enough for one standard 9-inch pie)

INSTRUCTIONS:

① Preheat oven to 350 degrees Fahrenheit (177 degrees Celsius). Using a sharp knife, hack pumpkin into several large pieces. Don't bother removing seeds, because baking will make them easier to remove later. Place pieces cut-side down on a baking sheet with edges. Bake 30 minutes to an hour. The pumpkin is finished when its flesh pierces easily.

② Allow pumpkin to cool enough to be able to work with it, and use a large metal spoon to remove seeds (set them aside for roasting). Scrape remaining flesh away from rind and discard rind. Purée flesh in blender or food processor, or with a food mill, adding water if necessary to help it blend.

③ To preserve extra purée, store in freezer containers for up to several months. Don't even think about canning it. According to the USDA, pumpkin cannot be canned safely at home due to its density and acidity—not even in a pressure canner.

CHEESE, CHIVE, AND BLACK PEPPER SCONES

The bold, savory flavor of quinoa is nice with the other savory flavors in these scones, but regular whole-wheat flour works, too. These are great in wintertime served with tomato soup.

If you make your own quinoa flour, you can add extra nuttiness by pretoasting the quinoa (see page 16).

YIELD: About 12 scones

INGREDIENTS:

¾ c. (83g) quinoa flour

1½ c. (120g) whole-wheat pastry flour

2 tsp. (10g) baking powder

½ tsp. (2.5g) baking soda

1 tsp. (4g) salt

1 tsp. (2g) nutmeg

Several twists freshly ground black pepper

1¼ stick (10 tbsp. or 141g) unsalted butter, cut into small pats or grated, and kept cold (ideally in freezer)

¼ c. (57g) cold cream, plus extra for brushing tops

¼ c. (57g) cold crème fraîche or yogurt

¼ c. (12g) chopped chives

2 c. (226g) grated Cheddar cheese

INSTRUCTIONS:

① Line baking sheet with parchment paper or silicone mat, or grease lightly with cooking spray. Place pan in freezer or refrigerator until use.

② In a food processor or mixing bowl, sift together flours, baking powder, baking soda, salt, nutmeg, and lots and lots of black pepper. Using your fingertips, two forks, a pastry blender, or the careful pulsing action of a food processor, rub or cut in butter. The smallest pieces should be no larger than a pea, and roughly half the flour should be coated in fat. Put bowl in freezer or refrigerator while you mix the wet ingredients.

③ In a mixing bowl, stir together cream, crème fraîche, chives, and all but a small handful of cheese (reserve some for topping). With a large spatula, fold wet ingredients into dry ingredients, just until combined. This is a good time to preheat oven to 375 degrees Fahrenheit (191 degrees Celsius).

④ Put a large piece of parchment or wax paper on counter. Dump dough onto it. Holding onto dough from the outsides of the paper, fold dough over onto itself a few times, attempting to form a 1-inch-thick rectangle. Chill dough in refrigerator at least 30 minutes, then cut into triangles with a sharp, serrated knife.

⑤ Arrange scones on chilled baking sheet, leaving an inch between them. Brush tops lightly with cream, then sprinkle with cheese and more pepper. Bake 22 to 25 minutes, or until deep golden on top, with crispy bits of cheese. (If using a cast-iron scone pan, preheat it while the oven preheats.)

WHOLE-WHEAT PIE CRUST

Practice makes perfect, but almost any homemade pies are better tasting than store-bought versions. According to Ken Haedrich, author of the book *Pie*, "You can become about 85 percent proficient as a pie-maker in short order. The other 15 percent you'll acquire over a lifetime."

So be patient. Make small tweaks with each new pie. Try different fillings each season. Get used to the feel of dough in your hands. The road to pie perfection is paved with lots of good (even delicious!) intentions.

Don't skip the vodka in this recipe—it's one of the secrets to the tender, flaky crust you seek. Food scientist Harold McGee explains that it helps push dough layers apart as it (mostly) evaporates in the oven. Meanwhile, the alcohol inhibits the formation of gluten, resulting in dough that's easier to roll out and more tender when baked.

Vinegar, buttermilk, and sour cream yield similarly tender results, but they add their own flavors. Feel free to swap vinegar for the vodka, and sour cream or buttermilk for some of the water in the ingredients list below. You may also substitute up to a third of the flour with another whole-grain or nut flour of your choosing.

Continued

YIELD: 9-inch pie crust (double the recipe for a double-crust pie)

INGREDIENTS:

2 c. (160g) whole-wheat pastry flour, plus extra for rolling

½ tsp. (4g) kosher salt

1½ sticks (¾ c./170g) unsalted high-fat butter or ¾ c. pastured lard, cut into small pieces and kept very cold, or a mixture (I prefer a 50/50 ratio of lard to butter.)

2 tbsp. (28g) vodka (or apple cider vinegar)

3 to 5 tbsp. (42 to 70g) strained ice water, as needed (or chilled buttermilk or sour cream)

1 egg white (28g), beaten (optional)

INSTRUCTIONS:

① In a food processor or mixing bowl, sift together flour and salt. Using a food processor, pulsed gently, or clean hands, begin to "cut in" or rub the bits of cold fat into the flour. Eventually you'll have a chunky mixture that looks like coarse sand, with about half the fat coating the flour. It's OK to have some slightly larger pieces of butter, but there shouldn't be many larger than a pea.

② Sprinkle vodka and 3 tablespoons ice water over butter-flour mixture. If using a food processor, pulse once or twice to bring the dough loosely together, then turn it out onto a clean counter. Use your hands to form dough into a thick ball that barely holds together. If necessary, add a tablespoon or so of water at a time, just enough to pull the dough together. For beginners, it'll be easier to work with dough that has slightly too much liquid, rather than too little; but beware that excess water toughens the finished product.

③ Shape dough into a circle flattened to about ¾ inch thick and 4 inches in diameter. Wrap in plastic wrap, and chill for a minimum of 1 hour, or preferably overnight. (You can also put the dough into a gallon-sized plastic bag and shape it into the disc while it's inside the bag.) Chilling dough ensures that the fat won't melt too soon, but more importantly, gives the whole grains time to absorb moisture. If using all butter, you may have to let your dough warm up for about 10 minutes before you'll be able to roll it out.

④ Lightly flour a clean work surface. Unwrap dough and roll it into a 10-inch round with a thickness of about ¼ inch. Ease up on the pressure as you approach the edge—you don't want the edges to be too thin. Don't worry about little cracks that develop as you roll. You can crimp together edges that crack significantly and use excess dough to patch any holes.

⑤ Carefully line a standard, 9-inch pie pan with the dough. One easy method is to roll dough on waxed paper or a silicone mat, then invert it over the pie pan with one fluid motion, gently settling the crust into place. Or you can gently fold the dough in half, lay it in the pan, and then carefully unfold it. Steal a bit of dough from an overhanging area to patch a hole elsewhere if needed. Trim overhang to ½ or ¾ inch and crimp or flute the edges all the way around the rim between your thumb and index fingers.

Prick, or dock, the crust all over with a fork or pastry docker to create vents for steam that will lift and separate flaky layers. (If you use a perforated pie pan—see page 54—there's no need to dock the crust.) At this stage, it is best to let the pie crust freeze overnight in the pan and bake it frozen. At the very least, put the crust in the freezer for an hour before baking.

⑥ Proceed with pie recipe and bake as directed, or "blind bake" the crust without filling. (Many recipes call for prebaking an empty shell to prevent crust from becoming soggy.)

BLIND BAKING (OPTIONAL):

① Preheat oven to 450 degrees Fahrenheit (232 degrees Celsius), ideally with a baking stone (or unglazed ceramic tile) on the next-to-lowest rack of your oven.

② Line crust with parchment paper (not foil, which can trap steam) and fill it with a layer of dried beans or pie weights to keep crust from puffing up too much (the beans can be used many times over). This step is unnecessary if using a perforated pie pan. (See "More Tips for Pie Perfection," on page 54.)

③ Bake frozen crust in preheated oven, on the stone if using one, for about 15 minutes.

④ Carefully remove parchment paper and pie weights. Dock crust once more, or if desired, use a pastry brush to paint the crust with a beaten egg white to create a barrier from juicy fillings.

⑤ Bake for another 3 to 5 minutes (until just barely beginning to brown) for a par-baked shell, or another 10 to 15 minutes for a fully cooked, golden-brown shell.

WHOLE-GRAIN VARIATIONS

• You may substitute up to a third of the flour in the Whole-Wheat Pie Crust on the preceding pages with another whole-grain or nut flour of your choosing. Tastes to try: Kamut flour is buttery; nut flour is nutty; and sorghum flour is slightly sweet.

• For a savory pie crust variation, substitute a third of the flour in the Whole-Wheat Pie Crust with amaranth flour, cornmeal, millet flour, or quinoa flour. Also mix ½ cup (50 grams) of grated hard cheese (such as aged Cheddar, Gouda, or Parmesan) plus a handful of chopped herbs into flour mixture.

Use a rolling pin to flatten flour and fat into "paint chips" that will create flakiness during baking.

More Tips for Pie Perfection

• Here's another way to work fat into flour effectively, from Shirley O. Corriher in *Bakewise*. Pour the recipe's flour and fat into a bowl, toss to combine, and freeze mixture for 10 minutes. Dump mixture on counter and roll over it with a floured rolling pin several times, until mixture looks like "paint flakes that have fallen off a wall." This extra step will produce hundreds of flour-coated flakes of fat. Scrape mixture back into bowl, freeze another 10 minutes, then proceed with adding liquid and forming a disc of dough to chill.

• I've fallen in love with the Chicago Metallic perforated metal pie pan that Corriher recommends. It's not nearly as pretty as my other pie pans, but it heats quickly because it is thin and highly conductive. Cooking quickly is another important step in keeping the fat in pie crust from melting before the structure is set. This pan also has several holes in the bottom that allow hot air to make an especially crisp bottom crust while preventing the crust from buckling up during blind baking. It does such a good job at this that no pie weights are necessary with this pan. Plus, it costs less than $20 on Amazon.

Perforated pie pans help keep pie crusts extra flaky.

• Why buy frozen pie crusts when you can make and prefreeze your own? As long as you wrap it well (plastic first, then foil), pie dough can be refrigerated for a few days or frozen for up to a month. If you bake a lot, save time by doubling, tripling, or quadrupling your recipe—especially around the holidays.

DOUBLE-CRUST MIXED BERRY PIE

You can use any combination of berries in this pie, but don't skip the apple. Its pectin helps thicken the filling, as does the tapioca starch.

INGREDIENTS:

½ c. (110g) granulated sugar

¼ tsp. (1g) salt

2 tbsp. (18g) tapioca flour (can be ground from tapioca pearls)

Approximately 5 c. (710g) mixed berries (blackberries, blueberries, raspberries, strawberries)

1 medium, tart apple (113g), peeled, cored, and grated or finely diced

Zest of 1 lemon or lime (3g)

1 tbsp. (14g) lemon or lime juice

2 tbsp. (28g) water

2 frozen, unbaked 9-inch pie shells (recipe on page 51)

1 egg white (28g), beaten

1 tbsp. (7g) coarse sugar (optional, for topping)

1 tsp. (4g) coarse or flaked salt (optional, for topping)

INSTRUCTIONS:

① Follow instructions on page 53 for blind baking a frozen pie crust.

② While crust is blind baking, whisk sugar, salt, and tapioca flour together in a deep saucepan.

③ Toss in berries, grated apple, lemon zest, and juice. Cook mixture over medium-low heat, stirring occasionally, about 10 minutes. Strain out fruit and put aside.

④ Cook berry juice that remains in saucepan about another 20 to 30 minutes, until thick and syrupy.

⑤ Spread fruit evenly into par-baked shell and cover with cooked fruit syrup.

Continued

⑥ Roll top crust into 10-inch circle. Cut a 1-inch circle out of the middle of the crust, or wait until crust is in place and use scissors to snip open three or four vents.

⑦ Cover pie with top crust, crimping edges together and trimming off excess overhang. (Alternately, cut crust into strips and weave a lattice.) Use a pastry brush to paint on beaten egg white in a thin, even layer. Sprinkle with coarse sugar and salt.

⑧ Return to oven to bake for 25 minutes, or until top crust is golden and juices are bubbling up in vent(s).

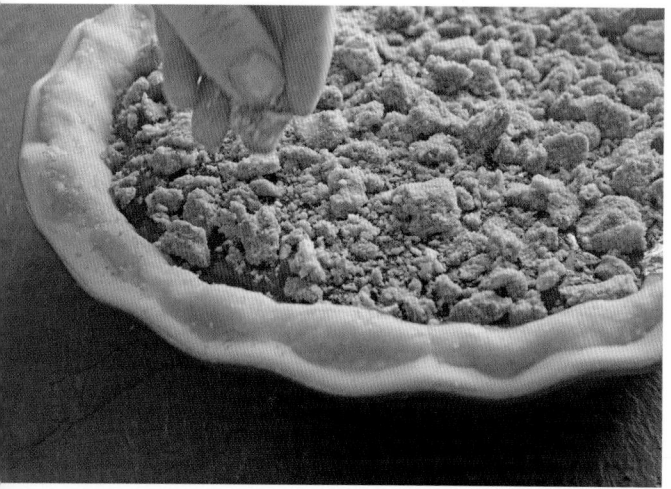

NUTTY CRUMB TOPPING

You may replace the top crust in a double-crust pie, such as the Mixed Berry Pie on page 55, with this buttery, nutty topping.

YIELD: Enough to cover 1 standard 9-inch pie

INGREDIENTS:

¼ c. (30g) favorite nut flour (You may grind nuts in a food processor, but be sure to use the pulse button and stop short of making nut butter.)

½ c. (62g) whole-wheat flour

½ c. (119g) brown sugar, coconut sugar, or granulated sugar

1 tsp. (2g) ground cinnamon

¼ tsp. (1g) salt

¾ stick (6 tbsp./85g) unsalted butter, kept cold, cut into small pats or grated

INSTRUCTIONS:

① In a food processor, sift together flours, sugar, cinnamon, and salt.

② Add butter and pulse a few times to combine roughly.

③ Turn out into a work bowl. Use fingertips to press together clumps of varying sizes, from pea- to grape-sized.

④ Sprinkle mixture over pie before baking.

CUTTING BUTTER into FLOUR, or the SECRET to FLAKINESS

There are many methods of smashing together fat and flour for biscuit, scone, and pie doughs. If flakiness is your goal, the most important thing is to keep the fat cold until baking time.

Biscuit, scone, and pie recipes typically ask that you "cut butter into flour," then add a small amount of liquid to help dough come together. As the pastry bakes, the fat melts and some liquid evaporates, pushing layers apart from each other with steam.

The process of cutting fat into flour can be accomplished with a variety of tools: two knives, two forks, a pastry fork, a pastry blender, or a food processor (if used carefully by pulsing but not overdoing it). The best method for a beginner, though, is to use your fingertips. Alton Brown, the Food Network chef who is a master of describing expert cooking techniques in layman's terms, describes this process as similar to rubbing a dog's fuzzy ears. Do it this way and you'll cultivate a better understanding of what good pie or biscuit dough ought to feel like as it rolls between your fingertips.

There is one cardinal rule to keep in mind with any biscuit, scone, or pie crust recipe: keep everything cold, and that includes both ingredients and equipment. If dough stays cold enough that its fat remains solid until time for baking, the fat will melt in the heat of the oven where it's supposed to, creating desirable separations—or flakiness—in the dough. To keep fat cool as long as possible, I cut butter and lard into pats then lightly dust them with flour to prevent them from sticking to each other. (A butter cutter is one of those unnecessary-but-useful tools that can make your life easier if this is something you'll do often.) I freeze these until it's time to work them into flour.

BUT WHAT IF YOU AREN'T LIKE EVERYONE ELSE?

If you prefer a tender pie crust without flakiness, simply combine fat with flour thoroughly. Do not attempt to preserve discrete pieces of fat or to keep them cold. You can even use warm oil. (My favorite fat for this purpose is coconut oil.) Make sure flour is well coated with fat before adding any water to prevent water from hydrating flour proteins and forming gluten. Basically, this is the opposite of the technique described above.

Chapter 5

YEAST AND WILD YEAST (SOURDOUGH) BREADS: FUN WITH FERMENTATION

HOW TO USE THIS CHAPTER:

This chapter of whole-grain yeast breads is organized into three parts. **That Famous No-Knead Bread** includes simple artisan bread recipes that are especially easy for busy people. Dig into **Infinitely Adaptable Whole-Grain Bread** when you want to go beyond the basics and explore more options for maximizing flavor. **Wild Yeast (Sourdough) Bread** tells you all about making sourdough, which is arguably the process best suited to whole grains. You'll find a lot of techniques that apply to all these types of bread at the end of the chapter.

Anyone can bake bread. Many are intimidated by the chemistry or have prior failures to thank for their trepidation. These days, most of us can't say we were lucky enough to have grown up knee-high to someone who baked. And of course, most of us believe we don't have time. But really, anyone can bake bread.

My aim with this chapter is to spread the message that all yeast breads are basically the same (different combinations of flour, yeast, salt, and liquid), and that there is a method of baking bread that will work for you. My hope is that after reading this and trying different variations, you'll have a better understanding of how to bake breads that *you* like in the manner that works most conveniently *for you*.

Besides learning a few basic bread-making techniques, you must also learn to trust yourself and allow yourself to be guided more by dough than by recipe. Your bread is a product of the techniques and ingredients you choose, the amount of time you let dough ferment, the temperature and humidity in your home, and the consistency (or lack thereof) of your oven, among a surprising many other variables. You must be confident in making adjustments based on these variables.

Culinary legend James Beard said all this best: "If you want to understand the art of bread baking, get your hands in the dough." This chapter can be your starting point. Get your hands in some dough!

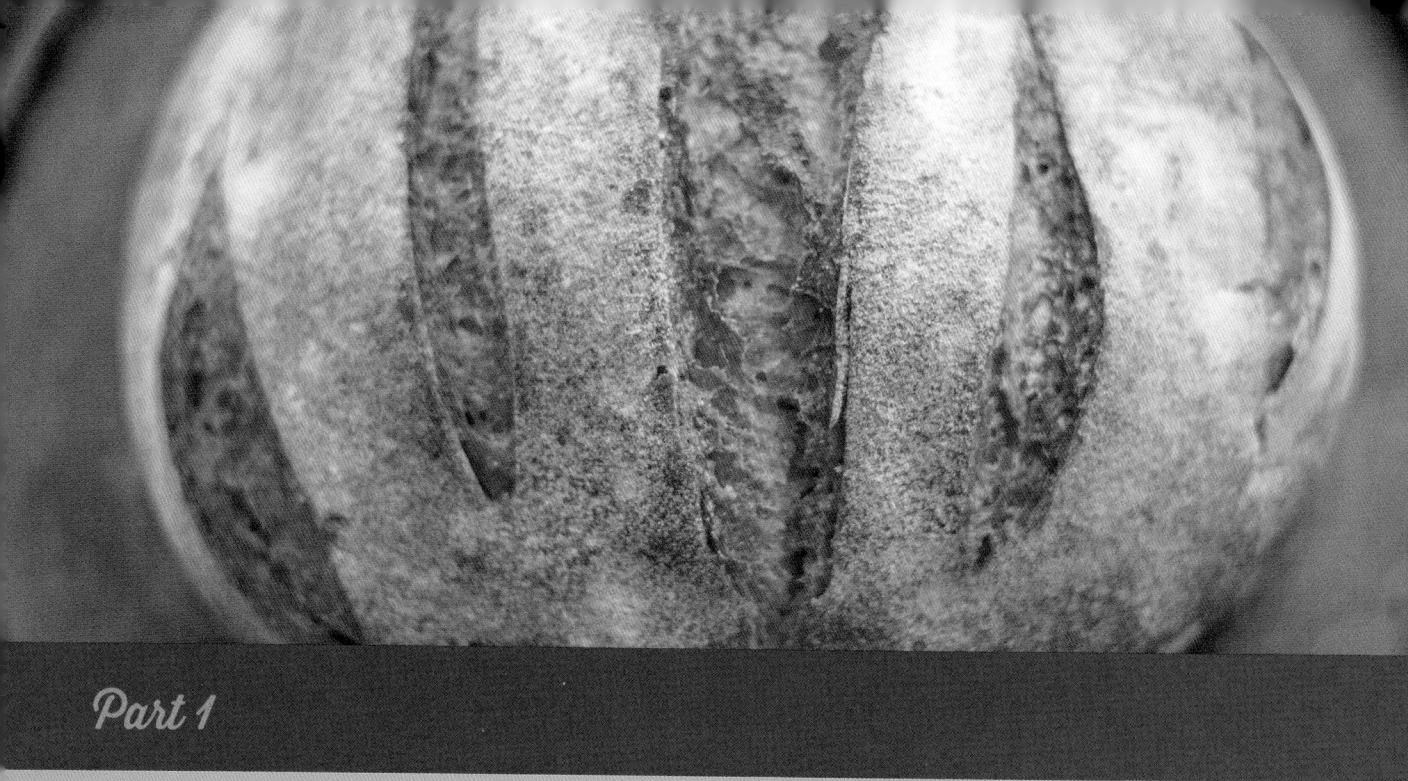

Part 1

THAT FAMOUS NO-KNEAD BREAD

Jim Lahey, founder of New York City's Sullivan Street Bakery and Co., an amazing pizza joint, has often been given the credit for popularizing the easy, no-knead method of baking bread that has taken the foodie Internet by storm. He and a couple of other bread experts, including Suzanne Dunaway, author of *No Need to Knead,* and Christopher Kimball, editor-in-chief of *Cook's Illustrated* magazine, recognized that making bread with very little yeast would encourage a long fermentation that would boost bread flavor. (To learn more about the benefits of prolonging fermentation, see page 97.) They also realized that really wet doughs could get strong all by themselves. This is because the gluten strands are more mobile and can align themselves without being kneaded in an effort to bring them into contact with each other.

BASIC NO-KNEAD BREAD

Here is the famous recipe Jim Lahey published in the *New York Times* in 2006. If you get a chance to visit his bakery or his pizza place in New York, you will not be sorry. You'll probably love his books too: *My Bread* and *My Pizza*.

YIELD: One 1½-pound (¾-kilo) loaf

INGREDIENTS:

3 c. (395g) unbleached all-purpose or bread flour, plus more for dusting (I use whole-wheat flour instead, and increase the water as needed.)

1⅝ c. (370g) cool water (about 60 degrees Fahrenheit or 16 degrees Celsius)

¼ tsp. (2g) instant or active dry yeast

1¼ tsp. (8g) salt

Cornmeal or wheat bran, as needed

INSTRUCTIONS:

① In a large bowl, combine flour, yeast, and salt. Add water and stir until blended; dough will be shaggy and sticky. Cover bowl with plastic wrap. Let dough rest at least 12 hours, preferably about 18, at room temperature (about 70 degrees).

② Dough is ready when its surface is dotted with bubbles. Lightly flour a work surface and place dough on it; sprinkle with a little more flour and fold it over on itself once or twice. Cover loosely with plastic wrap and let rest about 15 minutes.

③ Using just enough flour to keep dough from sticking to work surface or to your fingers, gently and quickly shape dough into a ball. Generously coat a cotton towel (not terry cloth) with flour, wheat bran, or cornmeal; put dough seam side down on towel and dust with more flour, bran, or cornmeal. Cover with another cotton towel and let rise for about 2 hours. When it is ready, dough will be more than double in size and will not readily spring back when poked with a finger.

④ At least half an hour before dough is ready, heat oven to 450 degrees Fahrenheit (232 degrees Celsius). Put a 6- to 8-quart heavy, covered pot (cast iron, enamel, Pyrex, or ceramic) in oven as it heats. When dough is ready, carefully remove pot from oven. Slide your hand under towel and turn dough over into pot, seam side up; it may look like a mess, but that is OK. Shake pan once or twice if dough is unevenly distributed; it will straighten out as it bakes. Cover with lid and bake 30 minutes, then remove lid and bake another 15 to 30 minutes, until loaf is beautifully browned. Cool on a rack.

ANOTHER VERSION

Ken Forkish, author of *Flour Water Salt Yeast*, uses a process similar to Jim Lahey's, but with slight variations. His recipe requires a third of the yeast, has 3 percent more water and calls for water that is 30 degrees Fahrenheit (16 degrees Celsius) warmer. He also employs the *autolyse* technique (discussed on page 103), and though he does not knead the dough, he does apply a couple of folds in the first hour and a half. It's a similar loaf, but it's not the same. It's incredible how tiny variables like this can change a simple loaf of bread.

AND YET ANOTHER . . .

Jeff Hertzberg and Zoë François have created five books' worth of big-batch recipes that allow you to make a bunch of dough (still with no kneading) that will last up to two weeks in your fridge. Whenever you want a loaf, you grab a hunk of dough, shape it quickly, let it rise, and bake it. Most of this work is hands-off time. They say it takes just 5 minutes a day, and it's not an exaggeration once you get used to the rhythm. Their big-batch recipes can be found in *Artisan Bread in Five Minutes a Day, Healthy Bread in Five Minutes a Day, Artisan Pizza and Flatbread in Five Minutes a Day, New Artisan Bread in Five Minutes a Day,* and *Gluten-Free Bread in Five Minutes a Day.*

NO-KNEAD CRANBERRY WALNUT BOULE

Cranberries and walnuts are a natural pair, and this is one of the favorite breads of our household. We got the idea to add black pepper to this recipe after trying a Jim Lahey walnut-raisin bread that contained a pinch of pepper. It's quite nice. This recipe showcases the flavors you can get from employing an autolyse (waiting awhile to add salt), and using very little yeast plus cool water for an extra-long fermentation (in the range of 18 to 24 hours).

YIELD: One 1½-pound (¾-kilo) rustic, round boule

INGREDIENTS:

1¼ c. (165g) whole-wheat flour

1¾ c. (235g) unbleached bread flour

¼ tsp. (1g) instant or active dry yeast

1¼ c. (285g) cool water (about 60 degrees Fahrenheit or 16 degrees Celsius)

¼ c. (57g) orange juice (from about 1 medium orange)

1½ tsp. (9g) salt

¾ c. (85g) dried cranberries

¾ c. (85g) walnut pieces

1 tsp. (2g) ground cinnamon

A few twists of freshly ground black pepper

INSTRUCTIONS:

① **Mix dough.** Add flours to a dough bucket or large bowl. Sprinkle yeast over flour evenly. Pour water and juice over flour, and mix with a dough whisk or your hands until uniformly moistened.

② **Autolyse.** Cover loosely and let dough sit for a 35-minute resting period, or autolyse. Sprinkle salt evenly over mixture and squeeze it into dough with wet hands, then cover container loosely.

③ **First rise.** About 30 minutes after incorporating salt, gently stretch and fold dough in its container, pulling up one edge at a time, just to the point of resistance but not tearing, and pull it back over the center of the dough.

Repeat until all sides of dough have been stretched. Cover loosely and let sit for another 15 to 30 minutes, or until dough has relaxed from previous folds. Stretch and fold dough all the way around once more. Cover loosely and let dough ferment until it's bubbly and at least doubled in size, 18 to 24 hours. (Note: You can omit the folding steps here if you are pressed for time. Just cover loosely and let it ferment.)

④ **Incorporate mix-ins.** Lightly flour counter. Use bowl scraper or flexible spatula to scrape dough out of bucket in one piece onto counter. Pat dough lightly into rectangle, and sprinkle evenly with nuts, berries, cinnamon, and pepper. Fold left side of dough over middle, then right side of dough over middle (like folding a piece of paper in thirds). Let dough relax for a minute. Now fold top of dough over middle, then bottom of dough over middle (again in thirds). Let dough relax again for a minute before repeating this business-letter folding process once more to distribute mix-ins throughout dough.

⑤ **Shape loaf.** Form dough into a round boule (pronounced "bool") by gently stretching four "corners" around and down to the bottom of the ball, pinching them together tightly at the bottom to hold surface tension. When shaping is complete, tuck any cranberries that are sticking out back inside dough so they won't burn in the oven.

⑥ **Second rise.** Transfer boule to a pizza peel or overturned baking pan dusted with cornmeal, flour, or wheat bran. (For more about these options, see page 90.) Cover shaped loaf with a floured towel, a slightly damp towel, or oiled plastic wrap to prevent a surface crust from forming. Allow to rise at room temperature for about an hour and a half. Again, it should be about 1½ times its original size and feel pillowy.

⑦ **Prepare to bake.** About half an hour before the end of the second rise, preheat oven to 500 degrees Fahrenheit (260 degrees Celsius) with a 5-quart or larger Dutch oven or other covered pan in the lower third of the oven.

⑧ **Slash loaf.** Lightly mist or brush the top of the loaf with water. With a swift, confident motion and a sharp, serrated knife or lame (bread-slashing tool), quickly slash top of loaf with ¼-inch-deep cuts. You can put an X across the center or make a few parallel slashes.

⑨ **Bake loaf.** When loaf is ready to be baked, using pot holders, remove hot pan from oven and uncover it. Transfer loaf into pan, and replace hot lid. Return pan to oven. Reduce heat to 450 degrees Fahrenheit (232 degrees Celsius). Bake 30 minutes. Remove cover and bake another 15 to 30 minutes, until deeply browned and firm.

⑩ **Allow bread to cool** on a rack for 45 minutes to an hour.

NO-KNEAD OLIVE ROLLS

The signature olive loaf at Tartine, a popular San Francisco bakery that makes sourdough breads, combines olives with walnuts, herbes de Provence, and lemon zest for a wonderful country bread. These no-knead yeast rolls boast the same flavors but are easier than sourdough to master.

YIELD: About 8 large rolls

INGREDIENTS:

1¼ c. (160g) whole-wheat flour

1¾ c. (240g) unbleached bread flour

¼ tsp. (1g) instant or active dry yeast

1½ c. (350g) cool water (about 60 degrees Fahrenheit or 16 degrees Celsius)

1½ tsp. (9g) salt

½ c. (55g) chopped, pitted olives

½ c. (52g) walnut pieces, roasted

1 tsp. (0.5g) dried herbes de Provence

Grated zest of 1 medium lemon (1g)

3 tbsp. (42g) unsalted butter, melted, for brushing on rolls

½ tsp. (2g) flaky salt, such as Maldon sea salt, for garnishing hot buttered rolls

INSTRUCTIONS:

Follow Steps 1 through 4 on pages 62–63, adding the olives, walnuts, herbs, and lemon zest (instead of nuts, berries, cinnamon, and pepper) during Step 4.

⑤ Shape rolls. Form dough into rolls by cutting off plum-sized pieces of dough with dough cutter or scissors. Quickly shape into balls by rolling each piece of dough around and around on counter until smooth. Or pull four "corners" of the dough down into a little knot at the bottom of each ball, then roll the ball on the counter to smooth out the pinched bottom. Don't worry about making them perfect—just aim to make little balls.

⑥ Second rise. Individual rolls can be placed on pizza peel dusted with cornmeal or in a greased baking pan to rise. Alternately, you can place them all into a greased 8- or 9-inch round cake pan or 9-inch-square baking dish with sides. At first they won't touch each other, but they should be touching after they have puffed up for the final rise. Cover rolls with a floured towel, a slightly damp towel, or oiled plastic wrap to prevent surface crusts from forming. Allow to rise at room temperature for about 45 minutes, or until pillowy and at least 1½ times their original size.

⑦ Prepare to bake. About half an hour before the end of the second rise, preheat oven to 375 degrees Fahrenheit (191 degrees Celsius) with a baking stone on the middle rack, if you have one.

⑧ Slash and butter rolls. With a swift, confident motion and a sharp, serrated knife or lame (bread-slashing tool), quickly slash the top of each roll with ¼-inch-deep cut. Or cut a little X into the center with scissors. Use pastry brush to paint melted butter onto rolls.

⑨ Bake rolls. Put baking sheet directly on baking stone and bake 20 to 25 minutes or until golden brown. Remove pan, brush with more butter, and sprinkle lightly with flaky salt.

⑩ Allow rolls to cool on rack for 10 minutes.

Part 2

INFINITELY ADAPTABLE WHOLE-GRAIN BREAD

Compared to the ingenious no-knead bread method featured in Part 1 (page 61), these breads take a little more (though still not much) active, hands-on time. I'll be honest: these loaves do require minimal kneading, and you'll dirty a few more dishes. Still, I love this technique, because it coaxes more flavors, more enzymes, more nuance, and better texture from your loaves.

The no-knead method works incredibly well with white flour and pretty well with whole-grain flour, but if you want to maximize the nutrition and showcase the deepest possible flavors of whole-grain breads, this method is the winner.

This method can also become just as adaptable to your lifestyle as no-knead bread baking. But again, I'll be honest: it won't feel like it at first. You'll read the steps and think there's a lot going on here. But after two or maybe three turns at it, you'll have a feel for the best way to fit the steps into your life—where to speed things up, where to slow them down.

Besides turning out more complexly flavored loaves of bread, the Infinitely Adaptable method teaches you some useful baking skills.

HOW TO BAKE INFINITELY ADAPTABLE WHOLE-GRAIN BREADS

The following instructions apply to all of the recipes on pages 70 through 79.

THE DAY BEFORE BAKING

Choose from among the recipes on the following pages to determine your soaker and sponge ingredients. Steps 1 and 2 can happen *up to 3 days before* you plan to mix bread dough, but be sure to do them *at least 6 hours before* you plan to bake.

① **Mix soaker.** Mix ingredients together. Cover and leave at room temperature for 6 to 24 hours. (You may also make this a few days before baking, in which case it should be refrigerated. Be sure to bring it to room temperature an hour before mixing dough.)

② **Mix sponge.** Mix ingredients together with wet hands or a stand mixer with its dough hook attachment. Knead or squeeze dough for about 2 minutes, then let it rest for 10 minutes. Knead again for about a minute. Cover and refrigerate for at least 6 hours. This can also be done up to a few days before use. (Note that you need to remove sponge from refrigerator about an hour before mixing dough.)

③ **Mix dough.** About an hour before you begin mixing bread dough, remove soaker (if it has been refrigerated) and sponge from refrigerator to allow them to come to room temperature. Add soaker and sponge, in alternating spoonfuls or handfuls, to the bowl of a stand mixer fitted with dough hook attachment (or a large bowl, if mixing by hand). Mix on low speed (or with wet hands or a dough whisk), just until everything comes together. Sprinkle yeast evenly around bowl. Add remaining ingredients called for in the recipe except honey, butter, and salt. Mix on first speed 2 minutes. Increase to second speed and mix another 2 minutes. Add honey, butter, and salt, and mix 2 minutes more. Let dough rest in bowl for 10 minutes. On a lightly floured work surface, knead dough by hand for just a few minutes, adding extra flour and water as necessary to create a soft dough that is strong enough to resist pulling yet is still malleable. Take care not to overknead if dough contains rye or spelt. Dough initially feels loose and sticky but gets stronger and more cohesive through resting, kneading, and shaping.

④ **First rise.** This stage is also called primary or bulk fermentation, because professional bakers deal with bulk batches. Form dough into ball and transfer it to a buttered or oiled bowl (or a clear dough bucket intended for this purpose), turning dough ball to grease it. Cover loosely with a lightly floured towel, oiled plastic, or the bucket's lid (not fully sealed), and let rise at room temperature for roughly 45 minutes. It should be about 1½ times its original size and feel pillowy and light. If at any point you must interrupt the rising process, simply retard dough by refrigerating it. Add about 20 minutes to its remaining rising time when you remove it. (You can also retard dough during its final rise (Step 10), but it is not advisable to do so both times.)

⑤ **Turn dough out onto floured work surface.** Using a dough scraper or flexible spatula, transfer dough to work surface in one piece. Let it rest for a minute. This allows gluten to relax, but also allows you to take note of the dough's structure. (If it seems strong and cohesive already, take care when shaping not to overwork it. If it seems slack and tears as you stretch, you may want to give it extra stretching folds before final shaping. If it's extremely slack, it's probably best to incorporate some more flour as you fold and shape, although generally you do not want to incorporate any more raw flour at this point.) After dough has rested for a minute, pat it lightly into a rectangle. Fold left side of dough over middle, then right side of dough over middle (like folding a piece of paper in thirds). Let dough relax for a minute. Now fold top of dough over middle, then bottom of dough over middle (again in thirds). Let dough relax again for a minute before repeating this "business-letter" folding process.

⑥ **Bench rest.** Rotate dough on an unfloured portion of work surface until a more-or-less round ball has been shaped; it does not need to be perfect. Cover loosely with a slightly damp towel to prevent surface crust from forming. Allow it to rest on a counter, or bench, for 10 to 20 minutes. The tighter the ball, the longer it will need to rest in order to relax enough to be shaped.

⑦ **Shape dough.** To form dough ball into a sandwich loaf, pat it into a rectangle, and roll it into an 8-inch cylinder. Tuck the ends in and under. It doesn't need to be perfect. The loaf pan will help it spread out. Place loaf in a greased 8½-by-4½-inch loaf pan or into a Pullman pan or other covered loaf baker. (Larger loaves can be baked in a 9-by-5-inch loaf pan.) Press any optional toppings gently onto top of bread.

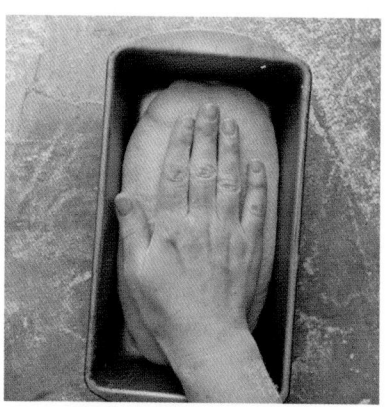

⑧ **Prepare to bake.** Preheat oven to 450 degrees Fahrenheit (232 degrees Celsius).

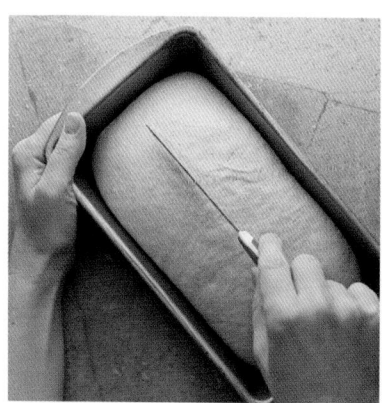

⑩ **Slash loaf.** Lightly mist or brush top of dough with water. With a swift, confident motion and a sharp, serrated knife or lame (bread-slashing tool), quickly slash top of loaf with a ¼-inch-deep cut down the middle. Slashing creates a place for the dough's gases to escape. If you don't do this, the dough will not rise to its fullest potential, and it will decide where to puff up all on its own. It probably won't be pretty.

⑪ **Steam oven (optional).** For a crisp crust and higher rise, humidify your oven via one of the methods on page 69.

⑫ **Bake bread** for about 40 minutes, reducing heat to 375 degrees Fahrenheit (191 degrees Celsius) after the first 10 minutes. If your oven has hot spots, rotate pan 180 degrees about halfway through baking. For help identifying when bread is done, see page 99.

Introducing steam into the oven during the initial stage of baking bread ensures a crisp crust and the best rise.

(9) **Final rise.** Cover loaf pan with a floured towel, slightly damp towel, or oiled plastic wrap to prevent surface crust from forming. Allow to rise at room temperature for about 45 minutes. Again, it should be about 1½ times its original size and feel pillowy. You may interrupt this process by retarding shaped dough in the fridge, but remember to add about 20 minutes to its remaining rising time when you remove it. (If you retarded it during the first rise (Step 4), it's best not to do it now.)

How to Steam an Oven

Enzymatic activity is quite lively during the first stage of baking. Starches are being converted into sugary compounds, and those on the surface of bread begin to brown and eventually caramelize. Adding steam to your oven during this stage is a great way to prolong the setting of the crust, which will give those compounds time to develop flavor. The steam also initially softens the crust so it won't weigh the loaf down, and this allows it to rise as much as possible.

I've tried a number of different methods to introduce steam into my home oven. By far my favorite method is to put a rimmed baking pan on the lowest rack of the oven (on top of a baking stone). Just before putting the loaf of bread into the oven on another baking stone that I have preheated on the middle rack, I pour ice or boiling water into the half-sheet pan and quickly close the oven. Of course, you must do all this as carefully as possible to avoid a steam burn. Any metal pan with short sides will work. I don't like to use cast iron, because the water can cause it to rust. And I don't like to use glass, because one time I stupidly put a cold glass pan into a hot oven, and of course it shattered on me. If you like, you can add landscaping stones to the pan. According to Shirley O. Corriher in the indispensable resource *Bakewise*, the stones will help trap and emit steam even longer.

Another option to try just before the bread goes in is to mist the oven walls with a spray bottle filled with water. You can also spritz the oven walls with a mister early during baking, but be fast and limit your spritzing to only a few times during the first 10 minutes or so. I don't recommend this option unless you have baking stones, which retain heat, in your oven. Otherwise, you may lose too much heat.

For an even crisper crust, prop the oven door open slightly with a spoon for the final 5 minutes of baking. If the loaf is in a pan, you can also (carefully) remove the loaf from its pan and allow it bake a final 5 minutes out of the pan. You can also increase crispness by baking a loaf closer to the top of your oven, but I don't recommend this unless you've already tried baking in the center of the oven and didn't like the results.

(13) **Let bread cool** on a rack for 1 hour before slicing.

BASIC WHOLE-WHEAT BREAD

This loaf contains only the fundamental ingredients: flour, yeast, salt, and water. But it is mixed in three different stages to maximize the flavor, texture, and nutrition you can get from different fermentation methods.

The entire process takes about 14 hours—wowza! But don't worry: almost all of this time is hands-off, and the process is extremely forgiving. If you need to stop at any point, the refrigerator is your friend. You can even delay mixing your dough for up to 3 days. It really is easy, but you must remember to make the simple soaker and sponge a minimum of 6 hours before mixing your bread dough—overnight is usually easiest.

Here we are following the time-tested method of creating parts of our dough in advance. There are many ancient methods for making these little predoughs, from Italy's *biga* to Poland's *poolish*. For this recipe, I love the method of separately mixing both a soaker (salt but no yeast) and a sponge (yeast but no salt) to coax different flavors and characteristics from the ingredients. If you find that you also like this method, you'll love the recipes in Jeffrey Hamelman's *Bread*, Peter Reinhart's *Whole Grain Breads*, and Laurel Robertson's *The Laurel's Kitchen Bread Book*. (To learn more about the science behind slow-rising bread—which will definitely make you a better baker—check out page 97.)

This 100 percent whole-wheat bread can be made with regular high-protein whole-wheat flour: hard red or white, spring or winter, so as long as it's not low-protein soft wheat. You can also use durum semolina, einkorn, Kamut, or spelt, or a combination of any of these. Read more about these types of wheat in the Whole Grain Glossary on page 13.

YIELD: One 1-pound (½-kilo) loaf

INGREDIENTS FOR SOAKER:

1¾ c. (219g) whole-wheat flour

¾ tsp. (4g) salt

**1 c. (227g) lukewarm water (not hotter than
100 degrees Fahrenheit or 38 degrees Celsius)**

INGREDIENTS FOR SPONGE:

**1¾ c. (219g) whole-wheat flour or unbleached
bread flour***

¼ tsp. (1g) instant yeast

¾ c. (170g) cool water

INGREDIENTS FOR FINAL DOUGH:

Soaker

Sponge

2 tsp. (6g) instant yeast

¾ tsp. (4g) salt

Extra flour and water, for adjustments

INSTRUCTIONS:

See page 66.

Commercial yeast is best stored in an airtight
container in the freezer and is most cost effective
if purchased in bulk.

HOW MUCH YEAST?

Note that the sponge in these recipes requires
¼ teaspoon yeast, and the final dough requires
2 teaspoons yeast. Together, this makes 2¼
teaspoons, which happens to be equal to one
standard packet of yeast. Purchasing yeast in
larger quantities to store in an airtight jar in your
freezer is more economical, but if you are using
a packet of yeast, take ¼ teaspoon out when you
mix the sponge. Put the remainder in an airtight
container and freeze it until you are ready to
use the rest of it in your final dough.

* Whole-grain flour absorbs more liquid than white flour. When adding liquid to bread dough, especially if you have changed the flour composition,
it's wise to add it a little at a time so you don't overdo it. You can always incorporate more liquid later.

EVEN BETTER WHOLE-WHEAT BREAD

In this variation on Basic Whole-Wheat Bread, butter creates a soft, airy crumb (interior) and slows staling; orange juice tempers tannins in whole wheat, which can seem bitter; honey sweetens a bit; and buttermilk adds a pleasant flavor and acidity, which also slows staling.

YIELD: One 1½-pound (¾-kilo) loaf

INGREDIENTS FOR SOAKER:

1¾ c. (220g) whole-wheat flour

¾ tsp. (4g) salt

¾ c. (170g) buttermilk, kefir, or yogurt (dilute extra-thick yogurt with water until pourable)

2 tbsp. (28g) orange juice

INGREDIENTS FOR SPONGE:

1¾ c. (220g) whole-wheat flour or unbleached bread flour*

¼ tsp. (1g) instant yeast

¾ c. (170g) cool water

INGREDIENTS FOR FINAL DOUGH:

Soaker

Sponge

¾ tsp. (4g) salt

2 tsp. (6g) instant yeast

2 tbsp. (43g) honey, molasses, brown sugar, or other sweetener

1 tbsp. (14g) unsalted butter, softened or melted and cooled

Extra flour and water, for adjustments

WHOLE-RYE BREAD

I used to think rye bread was so tricky. Rye doesn't contain much gluten, so you have to balance it with wheat if you want it to rise. Rye is like a sponge, soaking up more water than other grains, so you have to add more liquid. Also, it doesn't like to be overworked, so you have to be careful about kneading. And finally, rye is full of fast-acting enzymes that can wreak havoc on dough if you don't keep them in check.

Yes, rye is persnickety. But this recipe takes all those variables into account. There's extra liquid for the greedy bits of bran to drink up. There's acid to keep the enzymes in check (in the form of buttermilk as well as the acidity that develops during fermentation), and you'll add a little bit of rye flour late in the process instead of in the sponge, so it won't have as much time to do enzymatic damage.

Many people like to add vital wheat gluten to rye bread doughs to get the rise they want, but this loaf seems to do just fine without it—as long as you're careful not to overknead. (If you want to add vital wheat gluten, mix a tablespoon into the flour.) For help choosing rye flours, see page 13.

YIELD: One 1½-pound (¾-kilo) loaf

INGREDIENTS FOR SOAKER:

¾ c. (74g) whole-rye flour (also known as pumpernickel)

1 c. (125g) whole-wheat flour or unbleached bread flour*

¾ tsp. (4g) salt

1 c. (227g) buttermilk, kefir, or yogurt (dilute extra-thick yogurt with water until pourable)

2 tbsp. (28g) orange juice

INGREDIENTS FOR SPONGE:

1¾ c. (220g) whole-wheat flour or unbleached bread flour

¼ tsp. (1g) instant yeast

Scant 1 c. (198g) cool water

INGREDIENTS FOR FINAL DOUGH:

Soaker

Sponge

¼ c. (25g) whole-rye flour

¼ c. (31g) whole-wheat flour

2 tsp. (6g) instant yeast

1 tsp. (2g) caraway seeds (optional)

1 tbsp. (18g) honey, molasses, brown sugar, or other sweetener

1 tbsp. (14g) unsalted butter, softened or melted and cooled

¾ tsp. (4g) salt

Extra flour and water, for adjustments

OPTIONAL TOPPING

½ tsp. (1g) charnushka (also known as nigella seed)

* Whole-grain flour absorbs more liquid than white flour. When adding liquid to bread dough, especially if you have changed the flour composition, it's wise to add it a little at a time so you don't overdo it. You can always incorporate more liquid later.

OATMEAL BREAD

Oats in all their forms add a ton of moisture to bread doughs. Using cooked oatmeal makes the crumb (interior) of this loaf almost creamy. This is a great bread for sandwiches.

YIELD: One 1½-pound (¾-kilo) loaf

INGREDIENTS FOR SOAKER:

1¾ c. (220g) whole-wheat flour

⅔ c. (227g) cooked oatmeal, packed (made from ½ c./57g rolled oats cooked in ¾ c./170g water)

¾ tsp. (4g) salt

2 tbsp. (28g) orange juice

⅔ c. (150g) buttermilk, kefir, or yogurt (dilute extra-thick yogurt with water until pourable)

INGREDIENTS FOR SPONGE:

1¾ c. (220g) whole-wheat flour or unbleached bread flour*

¼ tsp. (1g) instant yeast

¾ c. (170g) cool water

INGREDIENTS FOR FINAL DOUGH:

Soaker

Sponge

½ c. (62g) whole-wheat flour

2 tsp. (6g) instant yeast

2 tbsp. (36g) honey, molasses, brown sugar, or other sweetener

1 tbsp. (14g) unsalted butter, softened or melted and cooled

¾ tsp. (4g) salt

Extra flour and water, for adjustments

WHOLE-WHEAT BREAD FEATURING YOUR FAVORITE WHOLE-GRAIN FLOURS

A homemade loaf of bread is a great place to sneak some specific nutrients that you may be lacking into your diet. For health-promoting ideas, refer to the Whole Grains Glossary on page 13.

The Basic Whole-Wheat Bread and Even Better Whole-Wheat Bread recipes on pages 70–72 are made with 3½ cups (438 grams) flour—half of which is in the soaker, half in the sponge. This variation replaces 1 cup (125 grams) of whole-wheat flour with 1 cup of the favorite flour(s) of your choosing—again with half in the soaker, half in the sponge.

A few flours have specific personalities that you should be aware of. For example, barley, oats, rye, and spelt soak up a lot of moisture; and rye and spelt do not like to be overkneaded. For more about individual grain personalities, see page 13.

YIELD: One 1½-pound (¾-kilo) loaf

INGREDIENTS FOR SOAKER:

1¼ c. (160g) whole-wheat flour

Approximately ½ c. (60g) favorite whole-grain flour, or a combination

¾ tsp. (4g) salt

¾ c. (170g) buttermilk, kefir, or yogurt (dilute extra-thick yogurt with water until pourable)

2 tbsp. (28g) orange juice

INGREDIENTS FOR SPONGE

1¼ c. (160g) whole-wheat flour or unbleached bread flour*

Approximately ½ c. (60g) favorite whole-grain flour, or a combination

¼ tsp. (1g) instant yeast

¾ c. (170g) cool water

INGREDIENTS FOR FINAL DOUGH:

Soaker

Sponge

2 tsp. (6g) instant yeast

2 tbsp. (36g) honey, molasses, brown sugar, or other sweetener

1 tbsp. (14g) unsalted butter, melted and cooled

¾ tsp. (4g) salt

Extra whole-wheat flour and water, for adjustments

* Whole-grain flour absorbs more liquid than white flour. When adding liquid to bread dough, especially if you have changed the flour composition, it's wise to add it a little at a time so you don't overdo it. You can always incorporate more liquid later.

BARLEY BEER BREAD

If you like mustard, sauerkraut, and sausages, this is a great, tender bread to complement those strong flavors and coarse textures. This loaf features the classic German ingredients barley, celery seed, and beer. I like to use a Märzen, which is the traditional Oktoberfest beer.

YIELD: One 1½-pound (¾-kilo) loaf

INGREDIENTS FOR SOAKER:

1¾ c. (220g) whole-wheat flour

¾ tsp. (4g) salt

¾ c. (170g) slightly malty beer, such as Märzen

INGREDIENTS FOR SPONGE:

1 c. (125g) whole-wheat flour or unbleached bread flour*

¾ c. (70g) barley flour

¼ tsp. (1g) instant yeast

¾ c. (170g) cool water

INGREDIENTS FOR FINAL DOUGH:

Soaker

Sponge

2 tsp. (6g) instant yeast

1 tsp. (1g) celery seed

1 tbsp. (18g) honey, molasses, brown sugar, or other sweetener

1 tbsp. (14g) unsalted butter, melted and cooled

¾ tsp. (4g) salt

Extra flour and water (or beer), for adjustments

MULTIGRAIN BREAD

There can be more, much more, to bread than wheat. Incorporating a variety of grains, nuts, seeds, beans, and legumes into bread is an easy way to bring new flavors and nutrients to a basic recipe. Want extra tenderness and even more protein and fiber? Add oats or barley. Need help regulating appetite, sleep, and mood? How about including some millet, which is a good source of tryptophan? Interested in protecting your heart with omega-3 fatty acids? Toss in some flaxseed or walnuts. Like strong flavors? Add amaranth, buckwheat, or teff.

Some grains and seeds can be added to bread dough as is, but many need to be softened by cooking. Softer and smaller items (amaranth, flaxseed, flours, rolled oats, sprouted wheat berries, sunflower seeds, etc.) can be added raw. Larger and harder items (buckwheat, grits, millet, quinoa, rye berries, wheat berries, etc.) should be precooked by being simmered in water until soft. You can also use quinoa *flour* instead of quinoa, corn *flour* instead of cornmeal, rye flour instead of rye berries, etc.

For this recipe, you will replace about 1¼ cups (160 grams) of the flour in the soaker with your own combination of cooked and uncooked grains. This is a great way to use up small bits of uncooked ingredients leftover from previous baking adventures. It's also an excellent way to use leftover cooked grains, such as the brown rice you had with your enchiladas last night or the oatmeal you didn't finish this morning.

YIELD: One 1½-pound (¾-kilo loaf)

INGREDIENTS FOR SOAKER:

½ c. (60g) whole-wheat flour

About ⅔ c. (160g) cooked and uncooked grains (try one of the multigrain mixtures on page 79 or make up your own)

¾ tsp. (4g) salt

⅔ c. (150g) buttermilk, kefir, or yogurt (dilute extra-thick yogurt with water until pourable)

2 tbsp. (28g) orange juice

INGREDIENTS FOR SPONGE:

1¾ c. (220g) whole-wheat flour or unbleached bread flour*

¼ tsp. (1g) instant yeast

¾ c. (170g) cool water

INGREDIENTS FOR FINAL DOUGH:

Soaker

Sponge

⅓ c. (40g) whole-wheat flour or unbleached bread flour

2 tsp. (6g) instant yeast (1 standard packet)

2 tbsp. (36g) honey, molasses, brown sugar, or other sweetener

1 tbsp. (14g) unsalted butter, melted and cooled

¾ tsp. (4g) salt

Extra whole-wheat flour and water, for adjustments

Continued

* Whole-grain flour absorbs more liquid than white flour. When adding liquid to bread dough, especially if you have changed the flour composition, it's wise to add it a little at a time so you don't overdo it. You can always incorporate more liquid later.

Add nuts, seeds, and other tasty superfoods to basic whole-wheat bread for amped-up flavor and nutrition.

MULTIGRAIN MIX NO. 1: BRAIN BOOSTER

¼ c. (24g) ground flaxseed

1 c. (40g) dried berries (blueberries, strawberries, raspberries, etc.)

⅔ c. (57g) ground almonds (almond flour)

⅔ c. (57g) ground walnuts (walnut flour)

MULTIGRAIN MIX NO. 2: PROTEIN POWER

3 tbsp. (20g) oat bran

1¼ c. (20g) wheat bran

2 tbsp. (20g) uncooked medium-coarse cornmeal

½ c. (40g) ground almonds (almond flour) or hazelnuts (hazelnut flour)

1¼ c. (60g) cooked soybeans, lentils, and/or quinoa

2 tbsp. (20g) cooked amaranth, millet, or rye berries

MULTIGRAIN MIX NO. 3: SUPERFOODS

¼ c. (56g) cooked oatmeal

½ c. (56g) dried goji berries

¼ c. (28g) raw cacao nibs

2 tbsp. (18g) hemp hearts

2 tbsp. (24g) chia seeds

Note: For more superfood ingredient ideas, check out Julie Morris' compendium of nutrient-dense foods, *Superfood Kitchen.*

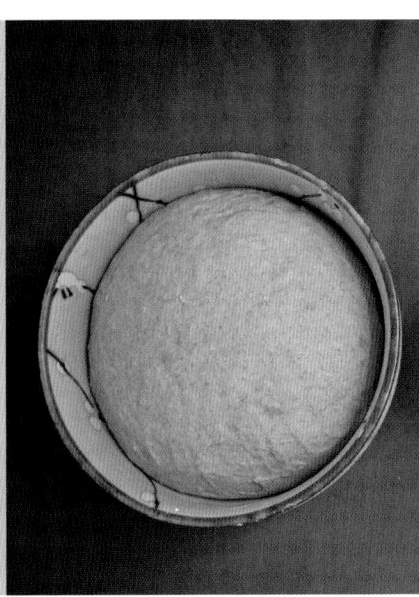

IMPROVING RECIPES

Making part of the bread dough in advance so that it will ferment more slowly will give you super-flavorful breads. To modify other yeast bread recipes to benefit from longer fermentation, begin your experiments by turning half of the flour, liquid, and salt into a soaker (left) and the other half of the flour and liquid—plus about 10 percent of the yeast—into a sponge (right).

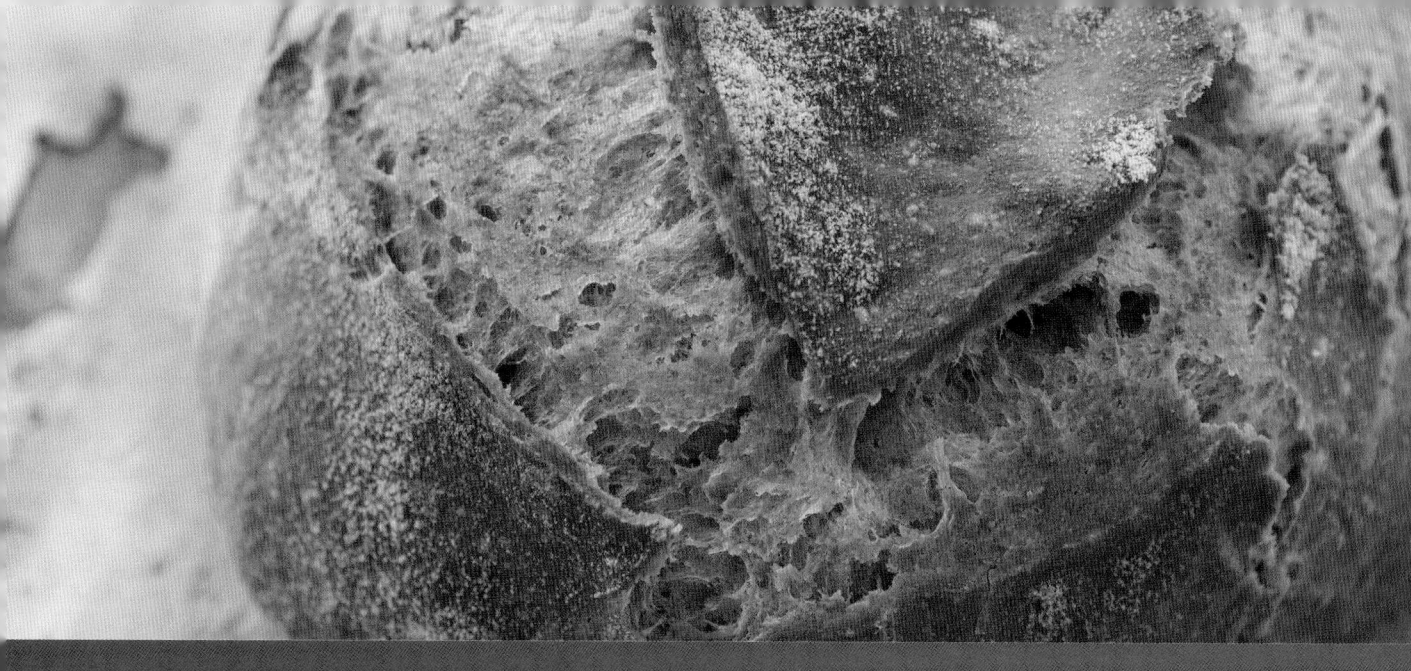

Part 3

WILD YEAST (SOURDOUGH) BREAD

For many people, the pinnacle of good bread is sourdough. Perhaps this is because more than 200 aromas can be detected in a well-made loaf. Lucky for anyone interested in this book, sourdough is probably the bread-baking method best suited for whole grains, because the complex ecology of a living sourdough starter works well with biologically complex, living foods. (The outer layers of wheat berries and other whole grains actually contain living cells.)

Yet many of these same people have shied away from trying sourdough at home. Sourdough recipes seem complicated because they involve steps that need to occur over more than one day, but the steps themselves are not complicated—sometimes nothing more than stirring is required. Even if you mess up here and there along the way, chances are good you will turn out tasty loaves.

There are a lot of different approaches to sourdough, which can contribute to confusion. With a little effort you'll both master the basics and find your own style . . . which is why, in this chapter you'll find tips from different experts about how they like to approach things.

You will not become adept at baking sourdough bread through reading alone. You need to see, smell, touch, and taste it to deepen your understanding in a meaningful way. This is true of all kinds of cooking but particularly so with sourdough, because you are caring for a living thing.

Amber Eisler, an instructor at the King Arthur Flour Baking Education Center in Vermont, says it helps to personify sourdough. "Sourdough likes to be at a comfy temperature. It likes to be fed regularly. It requires food, water, and oxygen, plus time to digest its meals. Think of it like a pet to make your life easier and sourdough bread less mysterious."

Sourdough Science

You don't have to grasp the science of sourdough in order to enjoy the bread, but trying to understand food chemistry is what makes many of us better cooks. A mysterious thing occurred when the microscopic lactobacillus bug befriended the wild yeast now known as Candida. However many thousands of years ago this occurred—some say it all started in Egypt around 1,500 BC—the symbiotic friendship that was forged would forever change our diet.

Just what exactly is happening in that bubbling crock anyway? A system of checks and balances between the two microorganisms keeps sourdough cultures healthy. Here's just a peek into the complex relationship: lactobacillus and other fermentation bacteria give sourdough culture its unique flavor. Candida yeast strains lift it up into a wonderfully airy loaf—crusty on the outside, chewy on the inside. The bacteria eat the sugars in flour that the yeast don't need, while the yeast eat sugars the bacteria don't need. The bacteria make the culture acidic, which creates perfect conditions for certain strains of yeast to thrive, and keeps competing bacteria out. The bacteria consume dead yeast cells, keeping the culture fresh. These and other checks and balances keep your sourdough culture strong for years and years.

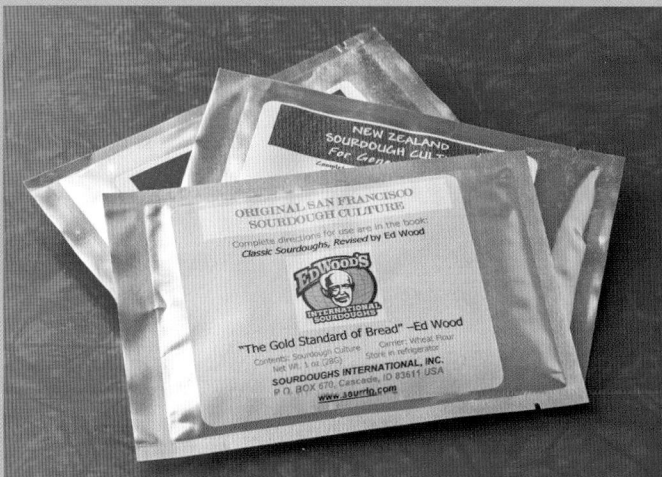

You can get sourdough starter from a friend who bakes sourdough breads or from a great online supplier like Sourdo.com.

BUBBLING GOO: GETTING A SOURDOUGH PET AND *KEEPING IT ALIVE*

OBTAIN A STARTER PET

Also referred to as a culture, *barm* (Irish), or *levain* (French), a sourdough starter is a mixture of flour, water, live yeast, and live bacteria that you will feed and perpetuate so you will always have enough to start, or inoculate, a new batch of dough. Each time you feed the starter, you encourage the proliferation of the microorganisms that leaven and flavor bread.

You can order starters in fresh or dried form from mail-order companies. (KingArthurFlour.com and Sourdo.com are two great sources.) These will come with instructions for refreshing or activating the starter. Usually the instructions tell you to feed the starter with equal weights of flour and water several times over at least a couple of days in order to bring it to full baking potential.

Feeding your starter helps its living microorganisms flourish so they can do the work of raising and flavoring your breads.

You can also get a sourdough starter from a friend or generous baker. Each time their starter is fed, they must discard some of the original batch. This discarded unfed starter can be used to make pancakes, waffles, and other goodies, or it can be fed separately, and thus turned into a new starter.

If you have an old sourdough starter that has been neglected, try to revive it at room temperature following the feeding instructions below before giving up on it. Start small and build it up a little at a time, once you notice that it is active again.

It is also possible to produce your own starter right out of thin air. The steps (see "Build a Brand-New Starter" on page 85) are simple but require patience, in addition to the willingness to give up and start over if it doesn't work right away.

Store your starter in a nonreactive (not aluminum, copper, or iron) container with an opening wide enough to allow you to stir inside it. Cover loosely, but make sure the lid is not airtight. Cheesecloth secured with a rubber band works well. KingArthurFlour.com sells a great sourdough crock with a nonairtight lid that keeps bugs and dust out.

DECIDE WHAT TO FEED IT

Some starters reportedly work best with either refined white flour or whole-grain flour. Through experimentation, you can discover which your culture likes best. Monica Spiller, a sourdough baker of more than 30 years and founder of WholeGrainConnection.org, recommends exclusively using 100 percent stone-ground whole-wheat flour for sourdough cultures. Many other bakers, for example Eric Rusch of Breadtopia.com, think white flour makes a better and more predictable starter, even if you want to use it to inoculate whole-grain doughs.

The reason whole-grain starters are more needy is that they are more alive. The enzymes in the outer layers and the germ of the wheat seed are not present in white flour. These contribute to more active and faster fermentation.

If you're using a starter purchased from a mail-order company, the recommended flour for feeding it should be noted on the instructions you received with it. If you received starter from someone else, ask what kind of flour they typically use to feed it.

FEED YOUR PET

About 8 to 12 hours before you plan to use your starter to mix dough, you'll need to feed it. Here's how. Discard half of it (it's OK to just eyeball it), and feed what remains with about 100 grams of flour (1 cup) and 125 grams of lukewarm water (just over half a cup). Stir to combine, and set starter aside for 8 to 12 hours to ferment before use.

For a milder-flavored sourdough (meaning it has less acetic acid), retain less original starter each time and feed it with more flour and water. Your breads will be closer to mild, fruity French levain breads than sharp, strong American sourdough breads. Vary the proportions until you find the flavor you like best.

LEARN TO IDENTIFY WHEN YOUR PET IS READY TO PLAY

A sourdough starter ready for baking is referred to as "fed," "ripe," or simply as "leaven." You can maintain a stiff starter similar in consistency to bread dough or a more liquid version. I like the lactic acid flavors I get from keeping a starter at a thick pancake-batter consistency; it's also easy to pour half of it out of my crock when it's time to feed it.

A classic sign that sourdough starter is ready is that it will float in room-temperature water. Amber Eisler of the King Arthur Flour Baking Education Center suggests also looking for the following signs.

- You should see small bubbles all over it (storing it in a glass jar will help to see the sides) and on top of it.

- Some small crevices also may have formed on top, which indicate that the mixture has reached its maximum volume and is beginning to sink.

- It should be aromatic, with a sourish-fruity smell, but not too vinegary.

THE SWEET NUTRITION IN SOURED DOUGH

The acids that build up in a sourdough loaf make it taste great and last longer than other kinds of bread, but their work doesn't stop there. These organic acids also make minerals and vitamins in flour more available than they might be in other breads and reduce the rate at which glucose is released into the bloodstream. This is why sourdough breads are rated lower on the glycemic index than other breads. The acids also make gluten more digestible—a concern for people with food intolerances. Recent research suggests that the transition away from long-fermented bread doughs might actually be responsible for the increase in gluten intolerance.

- It might look foamy in places.

- If using a stiffer starter, it will have domed and begun to fall.

You should ideally use starter to mix dough within about 2 hours of this "ripe" stage, give or take. If it has reached the point that it smells powerfully like vinegar and has fallen quite a bit, it will be better to feed it again than to bake with it.

Use your ripe sourdough starter to bake bread within a couple of hours of the peak readiness stage.

KEEP YOUR PET ALIVE

Now that you have an active wild yeast starter, you need to decide how best to keep it going. What works for you will depend on how often you plan to bake.

If you plan to bake sourdough breads just once or twice a week, it will be easiest to keep it in your refrigerator. Eisler suggests that you take the starter out of the refrigerator 3 days before you plan to bake and feed it a few times before you plan to use it.

If you will not be baking at all during the week or for a while, try to feed your starter at least once a week. Remove it from the refrigerator, feed it, and wait for it to reach optimal leavening power before you put it back in the refrigerator.

(Disclaimer: I once neglected my starter for about 10 weeks, and it came back to its former glory after just a couple of days of TLC.) It is possible to dehydrate starter for long-term storage too. Find an instructional video online at Breadtopia.com/drying-sourdough-starter-for-long-term-storage.

If you plan to bake three times per week or more, you're probably attentive enough to maintain a starter at room temperature, which is actually its ideal environment. In this case, feed the starter once a day. The day before baking, feed it twice without removing any starter the last time. There should be a minimum of 6 hours between feedings, and the last feeding should be a minimum of 6 to 8 hours before you want to mix dough.

BUILD A BRAND-NEW STARTER

For wild yeast breads, it all starts with the starter. You can purchase sourdough starters or use a bit of someone else's successful starter to inoculate your own batch. (Read more about that on page 82.) But it's fun to make your own live starter from scratch. It'll make you feel pretty proud to boot. You created a pet out of thin air!

When making a starter from scratch, keep in mind that it'll be about a week before you'll be able to bake any bread.

INGREDIENTS:

Whole-wheat flour

Warm water (filtered is best)

INSTRUCTIONS:

① Find a small, nonreactive container that allows plenty of room for expansion. Glass is great, because you can see what's happening inside it. Combine 100 grams of flour (about 1 cup) with 125 grams of water (just over ½ cup) in the container. Stir to combine. Cover jar with cheesecloth and a rubber band.

② Leave the jar on the counter for a few days, and stir vigorously with a chopstick several times a day for about 30 seconds at a time to aerate the mixture. Don't worry if you forget a few times, but try to do this at least twice a day. And use those times to observe and smell the mixture. If it looks dry, stir in a bit more warm water.

③ When you begin to smell a yeasty aroma (like beer) and notice some bubbles on the sides or top, your starter is ready for feeding. This means that wild yeast and bacteria have begun to ferment the mixture, and they will need more food to keep going.

④ Feed the starter once per day after this point by discarding about half of it and then stirring in 100 grams of flour and 125 grams of warm water until well combined.

TROUBLESHOOTING

If you end up with a starter that smells putrid instead of pleasantly sour, this is probably because you didn't aerate it enough, causing undesirable leuconostoc bacteria to proliferate. In addition to proper aeration, try bread expert Peter Reinhart's recommendation and start over using unsweetened pineapple juice instead of water. The acid should help control the wrong bacteria, allowing the desirable bacteria to thrive.

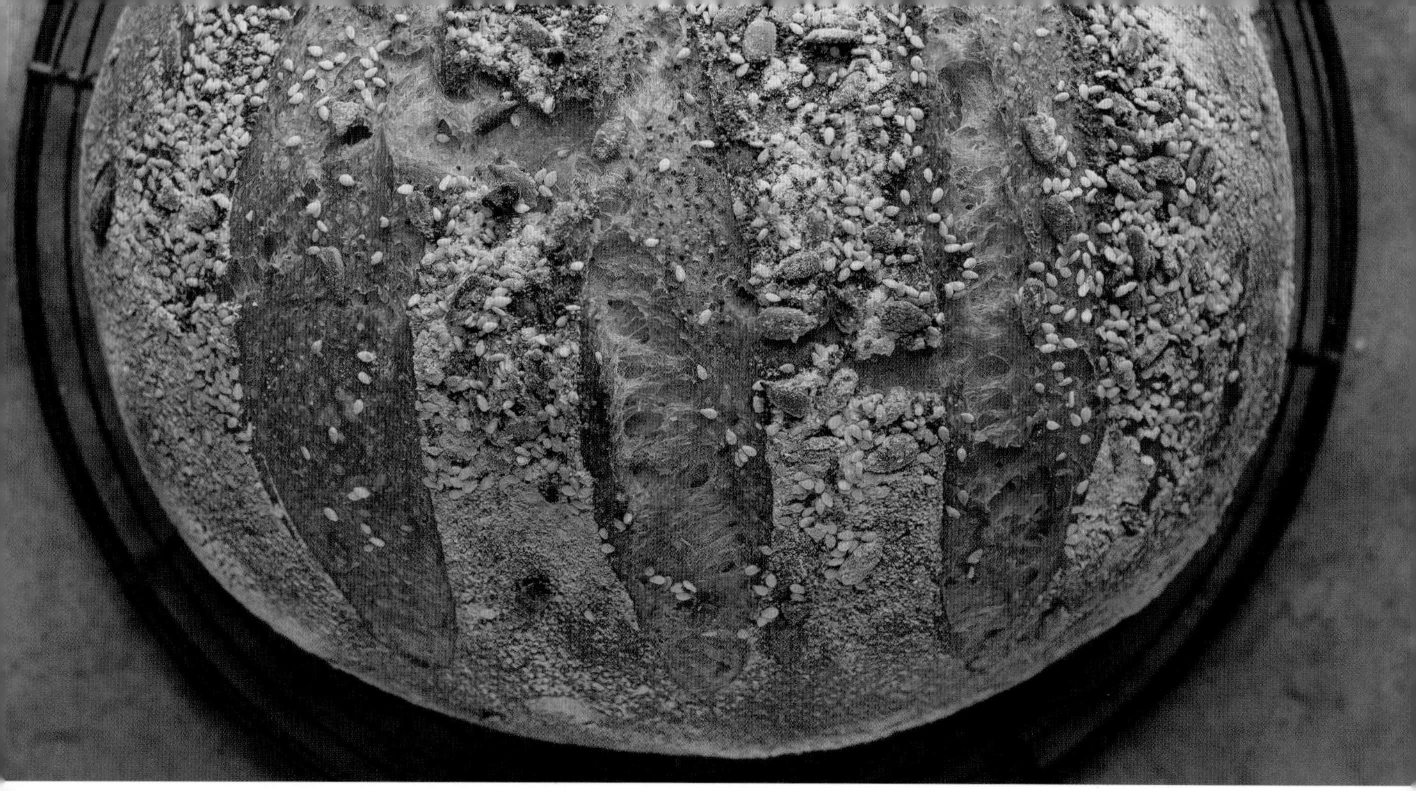

HOW TO BAKE WILD YEAST (SOURDOUGH) BREAD RECIPES

Sourdough recipes can vary quite a bit in terms of how much kneading is required. I prefer this method that employs an autolyse (see page 103) and involves just a little bit of kneading and folding to help strengthen gluten. You'll use this basic set of step-by-step instructions for all the recipes on pages 91 to 95.

① **Feed starter** according to the process explained on page 83. Allow to ripen for 8 to 12 hours.

② **Mix dough.** In a dough bucket or large bowl, pour ripe leaven into lukewarm water. I like to use a dough whisk for this process, but clean hands work too. Add flour, stir until loosely combined, then mix thoroughly with wet hands.

③ **Autolyse.** Cover container loosely and set aside for a 45-minute resting period, or autolyse.

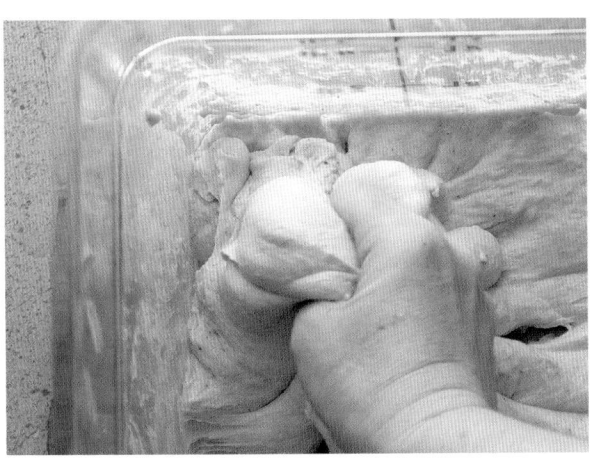

④ **Add salt and knead briefly.** Sprinkle salt over dough and mix in using wet hands. It should be sticky. If dough feels dry, add a little water. With wet hands, push, pull, and squeeze dough for a minute or two. Cover container loosely and leave at room temperature to undergo first rise. (Alternately, you may wish to use a proofing box set to a specific desired temperature; see "Own This Recipe" at 96.)

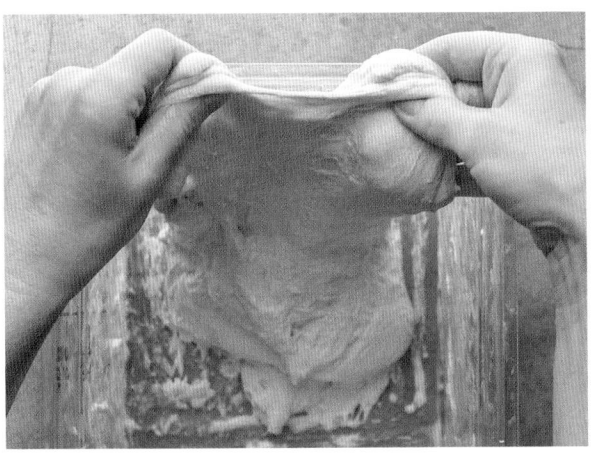

⑤ **First rise.** Allow dough to ferment at room temperature for about 3 to 4 hours, or another preferred time and temperature combo. During the first couple of hours, gently stretch and fold dough in its container, pulling up one edge at a time, just to the point of resistance but not tearing, and pull it back over the center of the dough. Repeat until all sides of dough have been stretched. Repeat this process about every 20 to 30 minutes, or until dough has relaxed completely from previous folding. After the first few times, be extra gentle and take great care to keep the built-up gases intact inside the dough. (Note: The first rise is one of two possible times that you can slow down the sourdough process by refrigerating, or retarding, the dough for up to 12 hours.)

⑥ **Turn dough out on floured counter.** Using a dough scraper or flexible spatula, transfer dough to work surface in one piece. Let it rest for a minute. This allows gluten to relax and gives you a chance to take note of the dough's structure. If it seems strong and cohesive already, take care when shaping not to overwork it. If it seems slack and tears as you stretch, follow this business-letter folding procedure once or twice: pat dough lightly into a rectangle. Fold left side of dough over middle, then right side of dough over middle (like folding a piece of paper in thirds). Let dough relax for a minute. Now fold top of dough over middle, then bottom of dough over middle (again in thirds). Let dough relax again for a minute before repeating this process once more.

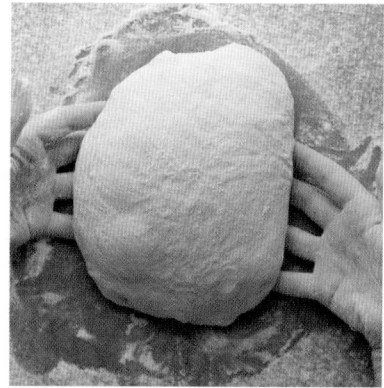

⑦ **Bench rest.** On an *unfloured* portion of work surface, rotate dough until a more-or-less round ball has been shaped; it does not need to be perfect. Cover loosely with a slightly damp towel to prevent a surface crust from forming. Allow dough to rest 10 to 20 minutes. The tighter the ball, the longer it'll need to rest in order to relax enough to be shaped.

⑧ **Shape dough** into a rustic, round boule by putting it on an *unfloured* portion of work surface. Spin it gently with your hands around the outside. The bottom will grab the surface and create tension as you rotate, stretching the outer skin. Another way is to hold the dough in your hands, gently stretch four corners to the bottom and pinch them together lightly. Either way, you're aiming for the ball to be fairly taut all the way around. Roll good side of dough (the side that will end up being the top of the loaf) in any optional toppings, or gently press them on top of bread.

⑨ **Prepare to bake.** Choose equipment for rising and baking (see page 90). If baking directly on a **baking stone**, preheat oven to 450 degrees Fahrenheit (232 degrees Celsius) with the stone in the lower third of the oven for at least 30 minutes. If baking in a **Dutch oven or other covered pan**, preheat oven to 500 degrees Fahrenheit (260 degrees Celsius) with the covered pan in the oven for at least 30 minutes.

⑩ **Final rise.** Depending on your baking method, let shaped loaf rise at room temperature upside-down in a floured proofing basket, which will help it keep its structure, or right-side-up on a pizza peel dusted with cornmeal or wheat bran. Dust a bit of flour on the surface and cover it with a kitchen towel to keep dough from forming a crust. The dough should take about 2 to 4 hours to proof at room temperature before being ready to bake. (If you prefer a different temperature, you may use a proofing box. See "Own This Recipe," page 96.) To learn more about recognizing when dough is ready for baking, see "Get to Know Dough" on page 99. This is also one of the two possible times that you can slow down the sourdough process by refrigerating the dough for up to 12 hours. Do not retard dough now if you did so during the first rise in Step 4.

⑪ **Slash loaf.** Lightly mist top of loaf with water. With a swift, confident motion and a sharp, serrated knife or lame (bread-slashing tool, pronounced "lahm"), quickly slash top of loaf with a few parallel cuts or a box shape. Slashing the loaf with approximately ¼-inch-deep cuts creates a place for the dough's gases to escape. If you don't do this, the dough will not rise to its fullest potential.

⑫ **Bake bread** according to method chosen below. If baking on a stone, shuttle loaf onto stone using pizza peel and bake for about 40 minutes. If baking in a covered pan, reduce heat to 450 degrees Fahrenheit (232 degrees Celsius) and transfer loaf to the pan. Cover and bake for 30 minutes. Remove cover and bake for about another 15 to 30 minutes.

⑬ **Let bread cool** on a rack for an hour before slicing. Sourdough is often better the next day.

Equipment for Rising and Baking

Specialty items help us bake excellent breads, but they aren't all essential. Chances are you already have something that will do the trick.

• To create a steamy environment—perfect for artisan breads with a crisp crust and soft crumb—bake loaves inside a covered **clay baker, cloche, or Dutch oven**. My favorite bread cloche is the gorgeous red one made by Emile Henry (emilehenryusa.com). I also love Lodge's combo cooker (lodgemfg.com).

• You can also bake bread directly on a preheated **baking stone**. **Unglazed tiles** from the hardware store work perfectly for this too—the thicker, the better. If you want a crisp crust on your loaf when baking directly on a stone, it's important to introduce steam at the beginning of baking with one of the methods detailed on page 69. Or you can slide a loaf onto the stone and then cover it with an **inverted pot** large enough to accommodate its full rise.

• If you plan to bake bread directly on a hot baking stone or in a covered pot, allow your bread to rise on a **pizza peel** (or overturned baking sheet) lightly dusted with cornmeal or wheat bran. This will make it easy to shuttle the bread onto the stone. For the purpose of dusting the peel, I keep a container of the largest pieces of wheat bran that I sift out of my freshly ground flour. My favorite peel, by far, is the innovative SuperPeel (SuperPeel.com). Another easy method when baking bread on a baking stone is to allow a loaf to rise on a piece of **parchment paper** or a **silicone mat** that can easily be slid directly onto the stone. To help the bottom of your loaf crisp up, carefully remove the parchment paper or silicone mat about 10 minutes before the end of baking.

• If you want an especially pretty loaf of bread, allow the loaf to complete its final rise in a shaped proofing basket, or **banneton**, lined with a floured cloth. (You can improvise a round banneton by lining a mixing bowl with a lightly floured towel.) With this method, you'll need to put the loaf upside down in the banneton during final rise (the nice side should be down and the rougher side up). When it's time to bake, invert the loaf onto the pizza peel, which will make it easy to shuttle into the oven. (You can also invert the loaf directly into or onto your baking vessel, but note that in this case, you need to slash the loaf *after* it has been placed in the vessel—not before.)

Top: Cast-iron sandwich loaf pan and perforated baguette pan. Center: Half-sheet baking pan, pizza peel, and proofing basket (banneton). Bottom: Enamel and cast-iron Dutch ovens.

BASIC SOURDOUGH

YIELD: One 1½-pound (¾-kilo) rustic, round boule

INGREDIENTS:

1 c. (227g) ripe leaven or fed starter

**1¼ c. (284g) lukewarm water (about 90 degrees
Fahrenheit or 32 degrees Celsius)**

**3 c. (375g) whole-wheat flour (or a combination of
whole-wheat and unbleached bread flour*), plus up to
1 c. (125g) more for the work surface**

1½ tsp. (9g) salt

INSTRUCTIONS:

Follow the instructions on page 86.

---

* Whole-grain flour absorbs more liquid than white flour. When adding liquid to bread dough, especially if you have changed the flour composition,
it's wise to add it a little at a time so you don't overdo it. You can always incorporate more liquid later.

SPELT SOURDOUGH

Spelt, an ancient grain, is sweeter, nuttier, and more nutrient dense than regular wheat. It has none of whole-wheat flour's bitterness. The almost no-knead method detailed in the instructions on pages 60 is perfect for use with spelt flour, because spelt does not like to be overmixed. Spelt flour also can drink up a good bit more liquid than regular whole-wheat flour, so I've upped the liquid here. Begin by using the least amount of water, and add more if necessary after the resting period (Step 3).

YIELD: One 1½-pound (¾-kilo) loaf

INGREDIENTS:

½ c. (113g) ripe leaven or fed starter

1¾ to 2 c. (397 to 454g) lukewarm water (about 90 degrees Fahrenheit or 32 degrees Celsius)

3 c. (300g) whole spelt flour (or a combination with some whole-wheat flour), plus up to 1 c. (100g) more for the work surface

1½ tsp. (9g) salt

2 tbsp. (36g) honey (if honey is thick, melt it and let it cool)

INSTRUCTIONS:

Follow the instructions on page 86. Mix in the honey at the same time as the salt, in Step 4.

NO-KNEAD SOURDOUGH

Eric Rusch of Breadtopia.com suggests substituting ripe sourdough starter for commercial yeast no-knead recipes (see page 60). Simply replace the ¼ teaspoon of yeast that is called for with ¼ cup (57 grams) of ripe sourdough starter. If you maintain a fairly liquid starter (pancake batter consistency), you may need to reduce the water in the recipe somewhat. You can always add more water later.

The popular no-knead method of baking crusty loaves of bread works just as well with sourdough starter as with commercial yeast.

KAMUT SOURDOUGH

Kamut has a wonderfully buttery flavor, and lends a pretty golden color to this loaf's crumb (interior). Like spelt, Kamut flour is highly nutritious and absorbs more water than most flours, so I've upped the liquid here. If you use a combination of Kamut flour and another flour, you may not need quite so much liquid. Always start with less water and add more later if needed.

YIELD: One 1½-pound (¾-kilo) loaf

INGREDIENTS:

½ c. (113g) leaven or fed starter

1¾ to 2 c. (397 to 454g) lukewarm water (about 90 degrees Fahrenheit or 32 degrees Celsius)

3 c. (390g) Kamut flour (or a combination of Kamut flour and whole-wheat flour), plus up to 1 c. (100g) more for the work surface

1½ tsp. (9g) salt

2 tbsp. (36g) honey

INSTRUCTIONS:

Follow the Basic Sourdough recipe on pages 86 through 89. Mix in the honey at the same time as the salt, in Step 4.

SOURDOUGH HAMBURGER BUNS

INGREDIENTS:

1 c. (227g) leaven or fed starter

1¼ c. (284g) lukewarm beer or water (about 90 degrees Fahrenheit or 32 degrees Celsius)

3 c. (375g) whole-wheat flour (or a combination of whole-wheat and unbleached bread flour*), plus up to 1 c. (125g) more for the work surface

1½ tsp. (9g) salt

1 egg white (28g)

¼ c. (57g) water

2 tbsp. (18g) sesame seeds (or other preferred topping; dried onions are nice)

INSTRUCTIONS:

① Follow the instructions on page 86 through Step 8, but instead of shaping one piece of dough, divide into eight pieces using a sharp knife or dough cutter and shape each into a ball. Place in baking pan or on baking sheet.

② With a damp hand, press down on each ball of dough to flatten it across the top. Cover with oiled plastic wrap, and let rise about 2 hours, or until nice and puffed up.

③ Preheat oven to 375 degrees Fahrenheit (191 degrees Celsius) with a baking stone, if you have one, on middle rack.

④ Beat egg white with water to make egg wash. Brush domed buns with egg wash, then sprinkle on sesame seeds. Press gently to help them adhere. With a serrated knife, make a quick slash across the top of each bun.

⑤ Put bun pan or baking sheet on the preheated baking stone, if using. Bake 16 to 18 minutes for regular-sized buns, or 13 to 15 minutes for sliders. The tops should be nicely browned.

⑥ Allow buns to cool on a rack for at least 15 minutes. Before serving, slice buns in half with serrated knife.

The difference between sourdough bread and sourdough buns is in the shaping. For perfectly shaped hamburger buns, use a bun pan (such as the individual pie and burger bun pan listed in the shop at KingArthurFlour.com, which can also be used to bake tiny pies). Or bake them on a baking sheet 1 inch apart.

Hamburgers are pretty tasty with sourdough that has been hydrated with beer instead of water. Try this recipe using a local pale ale instead of water for an interesting variation. I made them with Bronx Pale Ale (thebronxbrewery.com), and loved the results.

YIELD: 8 large hamburger buns or 24 slider buns

* Whole-grain flour absorbs more liquid than white flour. When adding liquid to bread dough, especially if you have changed the flour composition, it's wise to add it a little at a time so you don't overdo it. You can always incorporate more liquid later.

RYE SWEDISH LIMPA

With the aroma of sweet oranges and spicy licorice in your kitchen, it's particularly hard to wait for the cooling step, but don't skip it. It is always important to let breads cool if you want the best texture and flavor.

I like to use a little bit of all-purpose flour in this loaf to lighten it, but using 100 percent whole grain is great too. I also like a slightly less sour loaf with these flavors, so I don't let the dough ferment too long in either the first or final rise.

YIELD: One 1½-pound (¾-kilo) loaf

INGREDIENTS:

1 c. (227g) leaven (fed starter)

2 tbsp. (28g) unsalted butter, melted and cooled

¼ c. (71g) molasses

Zest and juice of 2 oranges

1½ tsp. (6g) anise seed

1½ tsp. (2g) fennel pollen (or fennel seed)

1½ tsp. (6g) caraway seed

1 c. (98g) whole rye flour

1 c. (125g) whole-wheat flour

1½ c. (195g) unbleached all-purpose flour, or more whole-wheat flour

½ c. (113g) water (about 90 degrees Fahrenheit or 32 degrees Celsius)

1 tsp. (6g) salt

INSTRUCTIONS:

① In a dough bucket or large bowl, pour in leaven. Stir in butter, molasses, orange zest and juice, anise, fennel, and caraway. Mix in flour. Add just enough water to form a smooth dough.

② Follow Steps 3 through 13 of the instructions on pages 86 through 89.

Own This Recipe

The Brod and Taylor proofing box makes it easy to use temperature to coax different flavors from your breads.

You can use time and temperature to your advantage in order to create a sourdough loaf of bread you love. If you follow the instructions in this chapter exactly, your dough temperature will end up between about 75 and 80 degrees, and it'll rise at room temperature. This should yield good rise and balanced flavor—not too sour. But you might want sourdough to be more sour—especially if you're a fan of San Francisco sourdough. In this case, a warm environment is your friend. Warmth encourages acid development and consequently acid flavor.

On the other hand, if sourdough is fermented in a cool environment, it will only be mildly sour, but other flavors of fermentation will be present, because cool environments favor bacteria over yeast. Many people prefer cooler-fermented breads, but this will take longer and may result in limited rise.

These and other variables explain the wide variety of fermentation times you'll see in sourdough recipes. The first rise may take anywhere from 2 to 12 hours. Yet it's also these variables that give you tremendous control over the final product. I suggest starting with the basic instructions on page 86, and begin adjusting from there. When you are ready to experiment, a proofing box, such as the cleverly designed folding proofer made by Brod and Taylor (brodandtaylor.com), is the easiest way to control temperature. In *Classic Sourdoughs*, author Ed Wood recommends undergoing first rise at approximately 70 degrees Fahrenheit (21 degrees Celsius) for the first hour, followed by a rather warm 90 degrees Fahrenheit (32 degrees Celsius) for the remaining time. This balance yields a loaf with mild sourness plus good leavening.

WHAT ABOUT ADDING COMMERCIAL YEAST AS "INSURANCE"? DON'T DO IT!

Some instructions for beginning a sourdough starter recommend adding a tiny pinch of yeast as extra insurance, just as some sourdough bread recipes you may encounter include commercial yeast in the ingredients list. This is unnecessary and potentially ill-advised.

Ed Wood, sourdough expert, author of *Classic Sourdoughs* and founder of Sourdoughs International (sourdo.com), cautions against ever adding any commercial yeast to a sourdough starter or sourdough recipe. "I definitely recommend not even having commercial yeast around," he says. "You might accidentally *contaminate* your sourdough culture with it. Yes, that's the right word." He explained to me that using commercial yeast in any amount—as so-called insurance—can simply mislead bakers into thinking the various fermentation stages have been completed when they have not.

PROLONGING FERMENTATION

Bread is a fermented food—just like sauerkraut, yogurt, chocolate, cheese, pickles, salami, and beer. This means bread is a product of the transformative action of microorganisms and the enzymes they make. On the quest for insanely good bread, one inevitably stumbles across techniques that prolong fermentation in order to let microorganisms create as many wonderful flavors as possible. All breads are fermented to some extent, but the more you can delay baking (up to a point), the more flavors you'll develop in the dough. Great breads can actually have the complexity of great wines—especially if whole grains are present.

Long fermentation probably sounds like something that's going to take *you* a long time, but that's not so. Giving dough extra time actually saves you time and trouble. Various methods of allowing this extra time include the French autolyse, levain, and *pâte fermentée*, the Italian *biga*, and the Polish *poolish*. In America, we often speak of pre-ferments, soakers, sponges, starters, sourdough starters, and, more recently, no-knead breads.

Typically, yeast breads are mixed and then kneaded in order to bring gluten strands into alignment, thereby creating the dough's eventual structure. It's then allowed to rise fairly quickly before being baked, and is often encouraged to do so even faster with extra yeast.

In most of the recipes featured in this chapter, you won't do much kneading. The fermentation time will do the structural work. You'll also let the dough or portions of the dough rest quite a bit, sometimes for a few minutes, sometimes overnight. These are moments when you can be doing something else, say, sleeping or making coffee. The overall hands-on time will be reduced and some of the bread's nutrients will be saved from the damages of incorporating too much oxygen through overmixing.

For an explanation of the science of bread flavor, we'll turn to Emily Buehler, who holds a doctorate in chemistry and has studied bread extensively: "Extra fermentation time results in more flavor, because there is more time for chemical reaction to occur, and the reactions produce the 'flavor molecules.'"

Long fermentation encourages the best possible flavor profile. The increased acidity also improves the gluten network, allowing for good shape, texture, and rise with less kneading, and it creates a moist bread that keeps longer than usual—without added preservatives. Most of the breads in this chapter will keep perfectly well for the

better part of a week. Using a wild yeast (sourdough) starter has the same benefits with even more pronounced flavors, but it requires more dedication.

People familiar only with dense loaves of whole-wheat bread will be glad to know that allowing more time to ferment also means you can use less yeast to raise the heavier grain. Too much yeast can cause a dense crumb with none-too-subtle flavors.

STANDING ON THE SHOULDERS OF GIANTS

In order to show whole grains in their best light, the recipes in this chapter use time-honored techniques from bakers past and present, especially the renowned French baker and professor Raymond Calvel; the experts at King Arthur Flour, in particular Jeffrey Hamelman; whole-grain guru Peter Reinhart; Suzanne Dunaway, author of *No Need to*

Long fermentation is the key to breads with complex flavor, with the added bonus of making the entire bread-baking process easier.

Knead; Christopher Kimball, editor in chief of *Cook's Illustrated*; and Jim Lahey, author of *My Bread*, all of whom helped turn America on to no-knead baking.

MIX-INS AND TOPPINGS

FLAVORFUL MIX-INS

Feel free to add 1 to 2 cups of flavorful bits to your breads, such as dried fruit, chopped nuts, pitted olives, grated cheese, caramelized onions, diced peppers, citrus zest, herbs, or other seasonings. Because these items can weigh the bread down, tear gluten, and occasionally decrease yeast activity, it's best to add them just before shaping dough for its final rise.

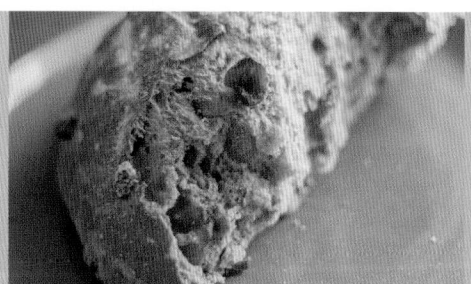

Cranberries and walnuts are a perfect pair.

CRUNCHY TOPPINGS

After shaping a loaf, but before it rises, roll the loaf in (or sprinkle on) finely chopped nuts; diced onions or shallots; anise, poppy, sesame and sunflower seeds; and whatever else you'd like to try. Charnushka (also known as nigella seed) is a traditional topping for rye breads. Mahlab, made from the pit of a cherry, is traditional on some Middle Eastern breads. Press toppings very gently into the dough with the palm of your hand or your fingertips to help them adhere better. Painting on an egg wash (¼ cup water beaten into an egg white) will also make toppings adhere nicely, but beware that it will darken the crust.

Toppings are a great way to add different flavors and nutrients to your baking experiments. Some of the world's best superfoods are tiny little nuts and seeds that are delicious on bread crust.

Technique

GET TO KNOW DOUGH

Learn when dough is ready to be shaped. When the first rise is complete, dough should feel airy and have a lightness to it. You may be able to feel some air pockets beneath the surface. It may reach this stage before or after a recipe's allotted time, and it may not have doubled, as many recipes indicate. I prefer to shape the breads in this book when the dough is roughly 1½ times its original size, although I have learned to pay more attention to the feel of it than its height. Amber Eisler of the King Arthur Flour Baking Education Center describes dough that is ready to be shaped as pillowy. She does not recommend the poke test that is popular in other bread cookbooks, as it can be too subjective. With time, you will learn when the dough's lightness is good and be able to catch it before it overproofs.

Learn when shaped dough is ready to be baked.
These signs are similar to when the first rise is complete. Eisler says the loaf should feel marshmallowy and light. It should have risen, though not necessarily doubled, but should not feel so fragile that it could deflate if you press on it. That would be a sign that it's gone too long, or become overproofed. Allowing dough to over-rise weakens its structure, resulting in smaller and misshapen loaves with a crumbly texture. The dough should be allowed to rise to its fullest extent *after* it goes into the oven. If dough has overproofed, bake it anyway. It will still be edible, and could still be better than a store-bought bread, but remember to catch it earlier next time.

Learn how to tell when bread is done. The classic thump test is still the best. If bread feels light for its size and sounds hollow on the bottom, it is probably done. The top should be deeply browned, not pale, even under the slashes. Eisler likes to try to squeeze the crust. If it yields to the pressure, it isn't done. It should be very firm until the bread cools down. (You'll have to remove bread from the oven to determine some of these variables.)

There are several ways to determine bread doneness. Thermometers are the easiest.

Always let bread cool to ensure best flavor and structure.

If you like to rely on temperature, make sure rustic loaves have hit at least 200 degrees Fahrenheit (93 degrees Celsius) internally. Sandwich loaves and softer breads should hit at least 190 to 195 (88 to 91).

Learn to let bread cool. The aroma of a fresh-from-the-oven loaf of bread is almost too intoxicating to resist, but cooling is as crucial as baking. If you want your bread to develop to its highest potential, don't mess it up right at the end. A period of rest on a cooling rack (between 30 minutes and a couple of hours for most breads; 10 to 15 minutes for small rolls) is essential to developing the final flavor notes. It's important for moisture, crust development, and structure too. The proteins are not quite done building the architecture until they cool.

BREAD EXPERIMENTS: TWEAKING VARIABLES

As you tweak different aspects of basic bread recipes—on purpose or not—you'll discover your preferred recipe. For example, you'll become familiar with the quirks of your oven and how bread dough behaves in different kinds of weather. You'll find out whether you prefer the flavors you get from cooler or warmer fermentations. With sourdough, you'll learn your starter's unique personality—what it likes to be fed, how long it usually takes to ripen after a feeding, and much more than you might imagine. As you try different recipes and experiment by tweaking variables, you'll gain knowledge and confidence. Here are a few tweaks you might try:

YEAST (AND WILD YEAST) VARIABLES TO ADJUST

- Sift out the largest bran particles from whole-grain flour before mixing dough. Use them to dust the pizza peel or proofing basket where the bread will rise. Or follow Michael Pollan's lead (from his latest book *Cooked*), and roll your dough in this separated wheat bran after shaping the loaf. This method can improve rise in whole-grain doughs, while retaining the nutritional benefits.

- Make dough that is wetter or dryer. Wetter doughs lend more air holes to the crumb, which most people love, but the dough can be more difficult to work with.

- Try recipes with different versions of kneading and not kneading.

- Adjust proofing temperatures up and down. This is easiest with a proofing box.

- Adjust baking temperatures up or down.

- Use different baking vessels, with and without steam in the oven.

- Slash dough in different places and in different patterns. Heck, slash your initials into the loaf if you want.

- Add various mix-ins and toppings.

- Replace the water with beer or cider.

- Try incorporating small amounts of different whole-grain flours.

Sifting out some of the coarsest piece of bran in whole-grain flour can lighten the flour considerably. Use the nutritious bran on the outside of your loaves, in muffin toppings, or anywhere else you like.

WILD YEAST VARIABLES TO ADJUST

- If you are used to light, white sourdough breads—and you like them—try sourdough recipes with unbleached bread flour instead of whole-grain flour first, using slightly less water. Begin swapping some whole-wheat flour for white flour with each new attempt to see how much you like best.

- Mix dough with more or less starter. Some doughs have up to 30 percent starter.

- Keep more of the original starter in each feeding for more sourness.

- Alternatively, keep less original starter at each feeding. The famous country loaf at Tartine Bakery in San Francisco begins with just a tablespoon of starter for a mild-flavored loaf. It is entirely possible to make breads that are naturally leavened but don't taste sour.

Find Time to Bake Your Daily Bread

If you are short on time, but like the occasional loaf of homemade bread, the best recipe for you is probably in Part I: **That Famous No-Knead Bread** (page 60).

If you love whole-grain breads with deep and complex flavors, and can manage to find a few minutes here and there to work on bread, try **Infinitely Adaptable Whole-Grain Bread** (page 66). The ingredients are adaptable, and so is the schedule—depending on who you are.

THE WEEKDAY BAKER

The easiest method for most people's schedules is to begin The Infinitely Adaptable Whole-Grain Bread recipe by mixing up a soaker and sponge (Steps 1 and 2) the night before you want to bake bread. It will only take about 5 minutes of active time. In the morning before work, mix dough (Step 3) and stick it in the fridge, covered loosely, to ferment slowly (Step 4). After work, shape and bake a loaf to enjoy for dinner (Steps 5 through 13).

THE WEEKEND BAKER

Make the soaker and sponge in the morning (Steps 1 and 2), mix and ferment dough in the afternoon (Steps 3 and 4), and shape and bake in the evening (Steps 5 through 13). To give yourself even more time, ferment dough in the refrigerator (Step 4) and bake the next morning (Steps 5 through 13).

If you are busy, but dedicated to the widest possible range of whole-grain flavors, you should definitely become a **sourdough** baker (see page 80). Here are a few sample sourdough baking schedules that might work for you:

THE SUNDAY AFTERNOON SOURDOUGH BAKER (USING REFRIGERATED STARTER)

- Friday morning: Take starter out of refrigerator. Follow the discard-and-feed process outlined on page 82, hereafter known as "feed starter."
- Saturday morning: Feed starter.
- Saturday evening: Feed starter.

TBSP	TSP	MILLILITER
16 Tbsp	48 tsp	237 ml
12 Tbsp	36 tsp	177 ml
11 Tbsp	32 tsp	158 ml
8 Tbsp	24 tsp	118 ml
5 Tbsp	16 tsp	79 ml
4 Tbsp	12 tsp	59 ml
2 Tbsp	6 tsp	30 ml
1 Tbsp	3 tsp	15 ml

Most people can squeeze baking projects into their life with a little advance planning.

- Sunday morning: Mix dough.
- Sunday late morning or early afternoon: Shape dough.
- Sunday late afternoon: Bake bread.
- Monday through Friday: Eat great bread.

THE WEDNESDAY EVENING SOURDOUGH BAKER (USING REFRIGERATED STARTER)

- Monday morning before work: Take starter out of refrigerator. Feed starter.
- Tuesday morning before work: Feed starter.
- Tuesday evening after work: Feed starter.
- Wednesday before work: Mix dough.
- Wednesday after work: Shape dough.
- Wednesday evening: Bake bread (perhaps in time for late dinner if rising place is warm).
- Thursday and Friday: Eat sandwiches.
- Saturday: Surprise your sweetie with French toast in bed.

Allow dough to ferment slowly in the refrigerator to give yourself more time.

THE FREQUENT SOURDOUGH BAKER, WEEKENDS (USING ROOM-TEMPERATURE STARTER)

- Every morning: Wake, brush teeth, put coffee on, feed starter.

- Every evening: After dinner, do dishes, feed starter.

- Saturday morning: Feed starter without discarding any starter.

- Saturday afternoon: Mix dough.

- Saturday evening: Shape loaf. Retard loaf in refrigerator.

- Sunday morning: Bake homemade bread. Impress brunch guests.

THE FREQUENT SOURDOUGH BAKER, WEEKDAYS (USING ROOM-TEMPERATURE STARTER)

- Every morning: Wake, brush teeth, put coffee on, feed starter.

- Every evening: After dinner, do dishes, feed starter.

- Morning before baking day: Feed starter without discarding any starter.

- Later that day, after work: Mix dough and let rise.

- Before bed: Shape loaf. Retard loaf in refrigerator overnight.

- Morning of baking day: Bake bread.

- Every day: Feel like a badass.

THE BAKER WHO RAN OUT OF TIME

There are two stages in yeast bread recipes where you can slow down the process, or retard the dough: during the first rise or after it has been shaped, during the final rise. The final bread will not have suffered. Many people actually prefer the flavors of colder fermentations. With either method, allow extra time after you remove the dough from the fridge. I do not recommend that you retard dough at both of these stages.

Lengthy Fermentation: A World of Ideas

• In the **autolyse** technique, generally credited to French baking professor Raymond Calvel, you mix flour with liquid to hydrate it fully before adding salt. This allows gluten to begin to structure itself and the enzymes present in flour to begin making various flavors. Salt slows down these reactions a great deal, so with this technique, we wait to add the salt—about 20 minutes for white-flour recipes and up to about 45 minutes for whole-grain recipes. *Soaking* flour overnight yields similar benefits, as does sprouting whole grains that have not yet been ground into flour.

• **Levain, leaven, and sourdough** generally refer to the same thing: a biologically complex and active wild yeast and bacteria starter.

• Biga, poolish, and pâte fermentée are variations on the theme of allowing a little bit of the recipe's total yeast, flour and liquid—but no salt—to begin to ferment. You can also call these by the more generic term *sponge*. A *soaker* also comprises only a portion of the final dough but typically contains a little bit of salt specifically to keep chemical reactions in check and usually no yeast. These processes elicit different flavors and textures. **No-knead breads** basically combine all these techniques into one

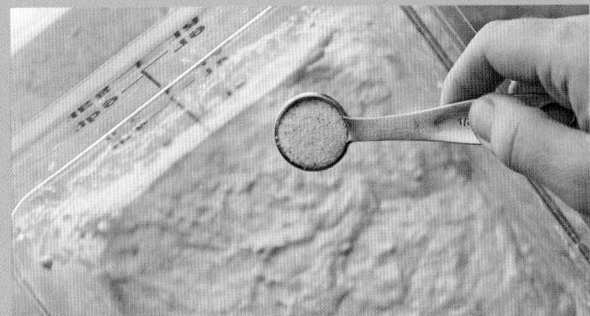

Giving flour a little bit of time to hydrate before adding salt helps develop extra flavor.

user-friendly recipe, in which everything is mixed together well in advance, but only a tiny bit of commercial yeast is included. Sometimes the refrigerator is employed to slow things down even further.

My favorite of these techniques depends on the bread I want to make, but I'd have to list sourdough as No. 1 in my book and making a bread from both a soaker and a sponge as No. 2 for flavor complexity.

Swap beer for water in traditional bread recipes for deeper flavor.

BEER BREAD

There's no reason bread must be made with water when plenty of other liquids hydrate flour quite nicely. Beer is a traditional liquid for bread baking, as brewers and bakers have a long history of working side by side. Cider, fermented (hard) or not (sweet), also works well in bread doughs. Many quick breads are made with beer, because beer's acidity works well with baking soda, but beer works well in yeast doughs too.

To make bread with beer or cider, simply replace the water called for in the recipe with the beer or cider of your choosing, or use part beer and part water. Experiment to see what flavors you like best. Recently, I loved the results I got from using the following beers in no-knead and sourdough recipes: Ananda IPA (Wiseacre Brewing Co.; Memphis, Tennessee); grapefruit Radler (Stiegl; Austria); Cherry Chocolate Stout (Stone Brewing Co.; Escondido, California); and my friend Nate's home-brewed hard cider.

Chapter 6

WHOLE GRAIN DESSERTS:
WHOLE INGREDIENTS, FULL FLAVORS

IN THIS CHAPTER:

I agree with Julia Child that we ought to enjoy everything in moderation—including moderation. These sweet recipes embody both principles. All are 100 percent whole grain and make use of a number of supremely healthy ingredients, including some healthful sweeteners. But there is definitely some sugar called for in the following pages. If you agree the occasional indulgence is acceptable, these recipes are for you.

To make desserts that are whole grain but still light and lovely, these cookies, cakes, and more rely heavily on expert techniques, the most important of which is using the right flour. Most of these recipes call for whole-wheat pastry flour, which comes from low-protein wheat that is much softer than the hard wheats we like for bread. Some additional grains with special tenderizing qualities also make an appearance. The dry ingredients are always sifted before use (easy to do in a food processor or with a whisk).

Additionally, mastering a few techniques—the creaming process, the egg foam process, and whipping cold cream—will improve the whole-grain dessert recipes you find here, as well as your overall arsenal of baking skills.

OATMEAL COOKIES with CHERRIES and WALNUTS

This cookie is oatier than most oatmeal cookies, with an interesting, hard-to-classify texture. The crunchiness of whole oats, walnuts, and flaxseeds is balanced by chewy cherries and tender pastry flour. Half the oats are chopped up, providing an in-between texture that pulls the whole cookie together.

YIELD: About 2 dozen cookies

INGREDIENTS:

1 c. (105g) chopped walnuts

1 c. (180g) dried cherries

2 c. (160g) whole-wheat pastry flour

1 tsp. (5g) baking powder

½ tsp. (2g) salt

1 tsp. (2g) ground cardamom

3 c. (240g) rolled oats (do not substitute quick or instant oats)

2½ sticks (1½ c. or 283g) unsalted butter, between 65 and 70 degrees

1¼ c. (298g) brown sugar or coconut sugar

½ c. (100g) granulated sugar

1 large egg (50g)

1 tsp. (4g) vanilla extract

½ c. (72g) brown or golden flaxseeds

INSTRUCTIONS:

① Line baking sheet with parchment paper, silicone mat, or a light coating of cooking spray or grease.

② In a dry sauté pan, toast nuts over medium heat, stirring and paying careful attention. (The moment you walk away is the moment nuts burn.) When nuts are fragrantly nutty and have a bit of brown sheen to them, immediately remove from heat to a separate container.

③ Chop cherries into bite-sized pieces. I like them cut into halves. Set aside with walnuts.

④ Combine flour, baking powder, salt, cardamom, and half the oats in a food processor. Process for a minute or two, until oats are chopped into small pieces.

⑤ Follow the All-Important Creaming Process on page 111 to cream butter with sugars, eggs, and vanilla. Now is a good time to preheat oven to 375 degrees Fahrenheit (191 degrees Celsius).

⑥ On lowest speed, stir in flour mixture, flaxseeds, and remaining oats, just until combined. Remove bowl from mixer. Gently fold in nuts and cherries.

⑦ Scoop ¼-cup portions of cookie dough onto baking sheet(s). This is easiest with a spring-loaded cookie scoop, or disher. Leave an inch between cookies. For cookies that are slightly crispy on the outside but softer in the interior, press dough balls down until they're about half an inch tall at edges, but slightly mounded in centers. For a crunchier cookie, press down until uniformly flat on top. Refrigerate pans for 30 minutes or freeze for 15 minutes.

⑧ Bake 12 to 15 minutes. Remove from oven when edges are browned and middles are slightly browned and no longer doughy. Let cookies cool on pan for 5 minutes before lifting them off with a spatula.

ALMOND BUTTER COOKIES

In addition to good-for-you almond butter and heart-healthy lard from pastured pigs, this homage to old-fashioned peanut butter cookies swaps whole wheat for white flour and coconut sugar for brown sugar. They may not replace your all-time favorite cookie, but I'll bet you have room in your heart for both.

YIELD: About 2 dozen cookies

INGREDIENTS:

1½ c. (120g) whole-wheat pastry flour

¼ tsp. (1g) salt (if using salted almond butter, omit extra salt)

1 tsp. (5g) baking soda

½ c. (85g) lard, preferably from pastured pigs (or unsalted butter between 65 and 70 degrees)

1 c. (238g) coconut sugar or brown sugar

1 large egg (50g)

¾ tsp. (3g) vanilla extract

½ c. (169g) plus 2 tbsp. smooth or crunchy almond butter

INSTRUCTIONS:

① Line baking sheet(s) with parchment paper, silicone mat, or a very light coating of cooking spray or grease.

② In a food processor or mixing bowl, sift together flour, salt, and baking soda. Set aside.

③ Follow the All-Important Creaming Process on page 111 to cream lard with sugar, egg, and vanilla. Now is a good time to preheat oven to 350 degrees Fahrenheit (177 degrees Celsius).

④ With mixer back to low speed, add almond butter. (Tip: It's easier to get sticky stuff out of measuring cups and utensils if they are lightly greased first.) Mix until well-combined, a couple of minutes.

⑤ On lowest speed, stir in flour mixture, just until combined, about 45 to 60 seconds.

⑥ Scoop ¼-cup portions of cookie dough onto baking sheet(s). This is easiest with a spring-loaded cookie scoop, or disher. Leave an inch between cookies. Take a large fork and press down across the middle of dough balls until flattened to about ⅓ inch high. Rotate fork 90 degrees and press again to form a crisscross. Dip fork in water between each cookie to prevent sticking. Refrigerate pans for 30 minutes or freeze for 15 minutes. This gives the fat time to firm up again and gives whole grains time to absorb moisture.

⑦ Bake for 15 to 17 minutes, or until cookies are deeply browned. To tell when cookies are finished, try this tip from the baking experts at King Arthur Flour: Open oven door and attempt to lift one cookie up with a spatula. If it buckles in the middle, it's not done. If cookie remains intact with a flat bottom, remove pan from oven. Let cookies cool on pan for 5 minutes to ensure they will be chewy.

NUT BUTTERS

All nuts can be ground into the buttery paste called nut butter. Roasting nuts before grinding them into nut butter adds a depth of flavor. Whole nuts are more expensive than nut pieces, and you don't need them for this purpose.

YIELD: ½ cup (scale up or down as needed)

INGREDIENTS:

Approximately ½ c. (125g) nut pieces

INSTRUCTIONS:

① Preheat oven to 325 degrees Fahrenheit (163 degrees Celsius). Pour nuts into a single layer on a baking sheet with edges. Roast for 5 to 15 minutes, paying close attention and shaking the pan around once or twice during cooking.

② Remove nuts when they have darkened and are fragrant but not burnt. Remove immediately to a separate container as they will continue to cook for a few minutes outside the oven. Allow them to cool before tasting—they'll be chewy while warm but crisp after they've cooled.

③ In a food processor, chop roasted nuts on low speed at first, then faster, until a cohesive mass of nut butter pulls away from the sides of the bowl. Some nuts become butter in less than a minute; some take several minutes.

COCONUT MOCHI MINI MUFFINS

Mochi is a Japanese dessert with a spongy-sticky texture all its own. We serve these little muffins at parties where everyone won't be seated, because they work well as finger food and are easy to make in advance. Every time we've served them, we've watched them vanish rapidly. They appear to be so small and simple, but quickly reveal themselves to be addictive. Everyone comes back again and again until they're wiped out.

You can bake regular-sized muffins instead, but then you wouldn't get the desirable ratio of as much caramel-y outside to chewy inside as possible. This ratio is key. You can also make these in a baking dish and cut them into squares, but it'll take a couple of pans, because you don't want the squares to be taller than about half an inch.

Mochi cake is traditionally made with mochiko, a refined flour made from short-grain *white* rice. Short grains of rice have more starch than longer grains, making them sticky or more effective as a thickening agent. But this useful property is true of short-grain *brown* rice too. It's much better for us, so let's use it instead, shall we?

YIELD: About 2 dozen mini muffins

INGREDIENTS:

1½ c. (188g) flour from short-grain brown rice (¾ c. whole rice, ground)

1 tsp. (5g) baking powder

¼ tsp. (1g) salt

1 large egg (50g)

1 egg yolk (18g)

½ tsp. (2g) vanilla extract

One 14-oz. can (scant 2 c. or 397g) unsweetened coconut milk

1¼ c. (200g) coconut sugar, brown sugar, or granulated sugar

¼ c. (54g) coconut oil or ½ stick (4 tbsp.) unsalted butter, melted and cooled

Zest of 1 lime (or 1 tbsp. dried lime peel)

½ c. (57g) shredded, toasted coconut

Optional topping: ¼ c. (28g) shredded coconut; 2 tbsp. (18g) black or white sesame seeds; zest of 1 lime

INSTRUCTIONS:

① Preheat oven to 350 degrees Fahrenheit (177 degrees Celsius).

② In a food processor or mixing bowl, sift together flour, baking powder, and salt.

③ In a separate mixing bowl, whisk egg and egg yolk with vanilla. Then whisk in coconut milk, sugar, oil or butter, and lime zest. Stir in toasted coconut.

④ Dump wet ingredients on top of dry ingredients and stir until just combined.

⑤ Pour batter into ungreased mini muffin pan(s), filling each cup halfway. Sprinkle sesame seeds, shredded coconut, and/or lime zest over the top of the muffins.

⑥ Bake for 20 to 25 minutes or until muffins begin to pull away from the sides of the pan. Cool at least 15 minutes before popping them out.

⑦ If there are any muffins left (there won't be), store in an airtight container in the refrigerator for up to 5 days.

SWEET BROWN RICE FLOUR

Sweet brown rice flour is one of the whole-grain flours in this book that you may not be able to find easily, because almost everything on the market is made from refined white rice. It's a cinch to grind yourself in a grain mill, however. Measure about ½ cup rice for each cup of flour.

TOASTED COCONUT

Preheat oven to 325 degrees Fahrenheit (163 degrees Celsius). Pour shredded coconut into a single layer on a baking sheet with edges. Roast for 10 to 15 minutes, paying close attention and stirring the coconut a few times during cooking. When coconut is lightly golden, remove immediately to a separate container.

FREEZING AND STORING COOKIES

Freeze individual balls of cookie dough for a fresh, hot cookie whenever you want one.

Cookies keep well for up to a week if stored in an airtight container after they've cooled. Remove air by sealing containers as you suck air out through a straw—a great tip from the King Arthur Flour baking experts. Baked cookies also freeze well this way for up to 3 months.

It's also easy to freeze cookie dough so you can enjoy just one or two freshly baked cookies any time you like, over a few months. There are two good methods.

① Roll cookie dough into a log inside parchment paper and seal in a freezer container. Cut off individual ½-inch-thick cookies with a sharp knife as needed.

Freeze individual balls of cookie dough for a fresh, hot cookie whenever you want one.

② Portion cookies onto greased baking sheets, and freeze the baking sheets for a few hours. When cookie dough balls are completely frozen, pop them into freezer containers or baggies. Portion out individual cookies as needed.

With either method, label containers with appropriate baking temperature and time. There's no need to pre-thaw dough. Just add a few minutes to the baking time.

Technique

THE ALL-IMPORTANT CREAMING PROCESS

Many dessert recipes—cookies in particular—ask you to cream some kind of fat with some kind of sugar. This process creates the nice, soft textures you seek and contributes a good deal of lift to baked goods, so it's an especially useful method when working with heavier whole-grain flours. Here are the basic steps.

(1) Get your fat(s) and eggs out of the fridge to warm up—but not too much. Eggs will incorporate into batters and doughs faster at room temperature than if they are cold. The best working temperature for fats is between 65 and 70 degrees Fahrenheit (18 and 21 degrees Celsius). If you're not using a thermometer, the fat should be just soft enough that you can make an impression in it with a finger, but it should not be anywhere near melting. If your kitchen is warmer than 70 degrees—very likely if you've been baking!—chill your mixing bowl and utensils until time of use. It helps to think of the target temperature for creaming as a cool room temperature.

(2) In the bowl of a stand mixer fitted with a paddle, or with a hand mixer, begin by beating the fat by itself first, on medium speed for about a minute, until it has coated the bowl and become a little bit fluffy.

(3) With mixer still running, pour sugar in slowly, beating until mixture becomes voluminous, about 5 minutes. Yes, that long! The texture will lighten as sugar cuts into the fat, creating fabulous pockets of air that will make your baked goods feel light. These air pockets are of utmost importance. Everything you do from here on should attempt to preserve them. Turn mixer off. (If at any point during the entire creaming process, the bowl no longer feels cool or you notice a look of oiliness, stop and put everything in the refrigerator for 10 minutes.)

(4) In a small bowl, beat eggs with vanilla (or other extracts). Egg whites contain water. Water does not mix well with fat. If you beat eggs before adding them to your fat-sugar mixture, emulsifiers in the yolks will bind up the water in the whites.

(5) With mixer on low speed, slowly pour in beaten egg mixture. Working slowly helps preserve those air pockets. Stop and scrape the bowl with a spatula as needed. Increase mixer speed to high and beat for 2 to 3 minutes. All this beating strengthens the bond between the ingredients and lets the gluey emulsifiers in eggs do their work. This is crucial if it is not your goal to have all the fat seep out later in the oven. You have probably had this happen to cookies at some point. That's because many recipes do not sufficiently explain the creaming process. That's why you're reading this page.

(6) Now that your all-important fat-sugar mixture has been sufficiently creamed into a pillowy fluff, you can move on to incorporating dry ingredients and other bits and pieces. Keep in mind that if you started with a creaming process, you should usually fold flour in gently, just until combined. You are not trying to coax strength from gluten. Think of the difference between a crusty baguette and a soft chocolate chip cookie. Do not overmix.

MEDITERRANEAN OLIVE OIL BUNDT CAKE

If you've never had an olive oil cake, you're in for a treat. The texture is wonderful, and as long as you use a mild-flavored oil, you won't taste it.

Semolina flour is ground from durum wheat. The semolina in stores is coarsely ground, ideal for pizzas and pastas. For tender cake, use your grain mill's finest setting to make fresh flour, or if using store-bought semolina flour, give it a whirl in the food processor before mixing the cake.

YIELD: 10-inch bundt cake

INGREDIENTS FOR THE CAKE:

½ c. (71g) pine nuts

1 c. (80g) whole-wheat pastry flour

½ c. (60g) finely ground durum semolina flour

1½ tsp. (7g) baking powder

½ tsp. (2.5g) baking soda

½ tsp. (2g) salt

3 large eggs (150g), separated, at room temperature

½ tsp. (2g) vanilla extract

Zest of 2 lemons (or 2 tbsp. dried lemon peel)

½ c. (113g) olive oil, plus extra for greasing pan

½ c. (100g) plus 6 tbsp. (75g) granulated sugar

⅔ c. (152g) ricotta cheese (or full-fat plain yogurt)

¼ tsp. (1g) cream of tartar

INGREDIENTS FOR THE GLAZE:

1½ oz. (3 tbsp./43g) limoncello (or substitute lemon juice for a nonalcoholic version)

Pinch salt

⅔ c. (80g) powdered sugar

INGREDIENTS FOR THE FILLING:

1 batch Balsamic Cherries (recipe follows)

INSTRUCTIONS:

① In a dry sauté pan, toast pine nuts over medium-low heat until fragrant and barely brown. Do not walk away or they will surely burn. Remove from heat.

② In a food processor or mixing bowl, sift together flours, baking powder, baking soda, and salt.

③ In a small bowl, beat egg yolks with vanilla and lemon zest.

④ Preheat oven to 350 degrees Fahrenheit (177 degrees Celsius) and prepare bundt pan. Grease pan with olive oil, then dust lightly with flour. (Other size cake pans may be used, but you may need to adjust baking time.)

⑤ In a stand mixer fitted with a whisk, or with a hand mixer, beat olive oil with ½ cup sugar about 3 minutes, until thoroughly combined. While mixing on medium speed, slowly pour in egg yolk mixture. Blend in ricotta for 2 to 3 minutes.

⑥ On low speed, gradually add flour mixture, just until combined. With a wooden spoon or spatula, gently stir in pine nuts.

⑦ In a separate bowl that is thoroughly clean and dry, using a balloon whisk that is thoroughly clean and dry, beat egg whites until foamy, about 30 seconds. Whisk in cream of tartar. Continue beating until soft peaks form, then slowly add remaining 6 tablespoons sugar, one at a time. The meringue is ready when stiff peaks stand up after whisk is lifted. Stir a large dollop of meringue into batter, then whisk or fold in the rest in a few big piles. Be gentle and stop when batter is uniformly combined. It's better to maintain volume than to mix too thoroughly.

⑧ Pour batter into bundt pan and smooth the top. Bake for 35 minutes, or until browned and set. A knife inserted into the cake should come out with no more than a few bits of moist, not wet, crumbs clinging to it. Invert bundt onto a serving platter or cake stand to cool.

⑨ While cake is baking, prepare lemon glaze. Whisk limoncello or lemon juice and a pinch of salt into powdered sugar. While cake is warm, drizzle glaze over top. There should be enough glaze to coat the cake in several passes.

⑩ If desired, fill center of bundt with Balsamic Cherries.

BALSAMIC CHERRIES

YIELD: This recipe makes enough cherries to fill the middle of the bundt cake above. Scale up if you'd like to have some left over for your morning oatmeal or yogurt.

INGREDIENTS:

2 c. (227g) pitted cherries, sweet or tart, fresh or frozen, with their juices

1 tbsp. (14g) aged balsamic vinegar

1 tbsp. (14g) honey (or sugar) for sweet cherries, or triple that for tart cherries

Tiny pinch ground cloves

Tiny pinch coriander

INSTRUCTIONS:

Simmer ingredients together over medium-low heat until liquid is reduced to syrup, about 15 minutes.

ALMOND-BERRY DARK CHOCOLATE CAKE

Despite containing whole-wheat and nut flours, this cake is velvety and light, owing to the tenderizing effect of olive oil and the addition of whipped egg whites and cream. Use the finest dark chocolate cocoa powder you can afford. Precut parchment paper circles and spring-form pans, such as those from King Arthur Flour, are a worthy investment if you bake cakes often.

INGREDIENTS FOR CAKE LAYERS:

1 c. (227g) strong brewed coffee

1½ c. (123g) dark cocoa powder

1 c. (227g) mild-flavored olive oil or coconut oil

2 c. (448g) superfine sugar (or 2 c. granulated sugar, ideally run through a food processor)

4 large eggs (200g), separated, at room temperature

1½ tsp. (6g) vanilla extract

1¾ c. (140g) whole-wheat pastry flour

½ c. (59g) almond flour or another favorite ground nut (Finely ground flour is best, but nuts ground in a food processor will work; use the pulse button and don't let them process long enough to turn into nut butter.)

1 tsp. (4g) salt

1½ tsp. (7.5g) baking soda

½ tsp. (2.5g) baking powder

1 c. (227g) very cold cream

¼ tsp. (1g) cream of tartar

INGREDIENTS FOR FROSTING:

3 c. (360g) powdered sugar

1 c. (82g) dark cocoa powder

¼ tsp. (1g) salt

¾ c. (170g) whole milk, at room temperature

1½ tsp. (6g) vanilla extract

6 to 8 tbsp. (85 to 113g) unsalted butter, cut into tablespoon pats, at room temperature

INGREDIENTS FOR ASSEMBLY:

6 oz. (227g) chunky berry jam or preserves

A few fresh berries

¼ c. (28g) slivered almonds

INSTRUCTIONS:

① Mix wet ingredients. In a small saucepan, bring coffee just to a boil. Turn off heat and whisk in cocoa until smooth. Scrape sides of pan down with a spatula. Set aside to cool. In a stand mixer fitted with the paddle attachment (or in a bowl with a hand mixer), beat olive oil and 1½ cups sugar on medium-high speed for a couple of minutes, until thoroughly mixed and creamy. In a small bowl, beat egg yolks with vanilla until well-combined. While mixing on low speed, slowly pour yolk mixture into oil mixture. Mix for a few minutes on medium-high speed, until thoroughly combined. While beating on low speed, slowly pour in cocoa mixture, until combined.

② Mix dry ingredients. In a food processor or mixing bowl using a hand mixer, sift together flours, salt, baking soda, and baking powder. With mixer on low speed, add dry ingredients to wet ingredients, a little at a time. Stop as soon as mixture comes together to prevent overdeveloping gluten.

③ Prepare for baking. Preheat oven to 350 degrees Fahrenheit (177 degrees Celsius). Prepare three 8- or 9-inch cake pans by lining the bottoms with parchment paper circles. (Springform pans are my favorite even though Food Network icon Alton Brown absolutely hates them—luckily, the choice is yours.) Grease the edges of the pans with lard, oil, or cooking spray, and sprinkle a light dusting of flour or cocoa powder over the grease.

④ Whip cream. In a clean bowl, whip cream with a balloon whisk or hand mixer until soft peaks form. Place the whipped cream in the refrigerator to keep cold.

⑤ **Make egg white foam.** In a separate bowl that is thoroughly clean and dry, using a balloon whisk that is thoroughly clean and dry, beat egg whites until foamy, about 30 seconds. Whisk in cream of tartar. Continue beating until soft peaks form, then slowly add remaining ½ cup sugar, one tablespoon at a time. The foam is ready when stiff peaks stand up after whisk is lifted.

⑥ **Incorporate foam and cream into batter.** With a large spatula, fold egg white foam and whipped cream into cake batter by alternating each addition in big piles. Be gentle and stop when batter is uniformly combined. It's better to maintain volume than to mix too thoroughly.

⑦ **Bake.** Pour a third of the batter into each pan. Tap pans gently to distribute evenly. Place pans on oven's middle rack. If they won't fit on one rack or if your oven has bad hot spots, alternate pans halfway through baking, using a steady hand to avoid sloshing cake batter around. Bake 20 to 25 minutes or until a toothpick inserted into the center comes out clean except for a few moist crumbs. The cakes should smell strongly of chocolate before they are finished. Allow cakes to cool at least 15 minutes in the pans set on a cooling rack. Then carefully invert cakes from their pans onto separate plates to chill or freeze before frosting.

⑧ **Make frosting.** Sift together powdered sugar, cocoa powder, and salt with a whisk. Whisk in milk and vanilla until thoroughly combined. Whisk in butter one pat at a time, waiting to add another until the previous butter has been incorporated. There should be no lumps in the finished frosting.

⑨ **Assemble layer cake.** Place one cold cake layer onto a serving plate or cake stand. Coat with a layer of frosting ¼-inch thick. Spread half the jam over the frosting. Repeat with second layer. Place third layer on top. Frost cake all over the top and sides. Sprinkle top with almonds and place a small bunch of berries in the center.

MAKE DARK CHOCOLATE CUPCAKES INSTEAD

Use this cake batter to make about 28 cupcakes. Fill each cup ⅔ full and bake for about 18 to 20 minutes or until the cupcakes pass the same tests as in Step 7 above. Cool pan(s) on a rack for 15 minutes, then gently lift out cupcakes and let them cool completely on the rack or in the refrigerator before frosting.

JUPITER CAKE

For my son, Jupiter's, first birthday, I wanted a knock-out cake. But a baby's first cake is not really for the baby; it's for the parents. So actually, I wanted to bake something special for us, which is why I decided to make a whole-grain twist on a recipe from the *Momofuku Milk Bar* cookbook. Momofuku Milk Bar in New York City is one of my favorite places to eat sweet stuff, and I am not alone. The concoctions coming out of Chef Christina Tosi's brain are innovative and unforgettable.

So I took Tosi's recipe for Chocolate Chip Layer Cake and repurposed it to fit my whole-grain way of thinking. This ridiculous cake is composed of four parts: a vanilla cake studded with chocolate chips; thick passionfruit curd; fluffy coffee frosting; and crunchy chocolate crumbs. I replaced all the flour in Tosi's recipes with whole-grain flours and most of the sugar with coconut sugar. So in addition to the intense flavors of passionfruit, coffee, vanilla, and chocolate, with the Jupiter Cake you also get the nutty flavors of freshly ground whole grains and the lightly caramel taste of coconut sugar.

A cake composed in four parts is no small project. If you don't often have time for an all-day baking adventure, you'll be relieved to know that everything can be made in advance without compromising quality. In fact, why not stretch the process out over a week so you can brag about the week-long cake you made for someone truly special? When we served this cake at our son's birthday party, one friend said the best thing about this cake is that it *looks* like it took a lot of work to make, and that made it even more enjoyable to eat.

Note: If you find yourself in New York City, you should absolutely abandon your whole-grain principles and treat yourself to anything at all from Milk Bar.

SPECIAL EQUIPMENT

Milk Bar cakes are presented unusually with gorgeous layers that proudly display the insides of the cake—no frosting around the outside. To build a bakery-display beauty like this, you'll need two pieces of special equipment, both available on Amazon.com. A 6-inch **cake ring** helps contain the tower of many layers in a circle while the cake sets. A ring of **acetate** placed inside the cake ring (this is also called a cake collar) makes it easy to build a cake as tall as you like. The strip of acetate should be at least 4 inches wide/tall and at least 20 inches long (to form a circle with some overlap; a longer piece will work). It's easy to slide the cake out of the ring and peel off the acetate after you freeze the cake for a few hours.

If you prefer to use whatever's in your kitchen right now, you can still compose an artful cake. In Step 1, grab a knife and cut the sheet cake into three equal rectangles. Compose the layer cake freestyle on a serving dish.

YIELD: 1 exquisite cake

INGREDIENTS:

1 Whole-Wheat Chocolate Chip Cake (page 118)

1 batch Coffee Frosting (page 119)

1 batch Passionfruit or Orange Curd (page 120)

1 batch Barley Chocolate Crumbs (page 121)

¼ c. (43g) mini chocolate chips

INSTRUCTIONS:

① Using a 6-inch cake ring, stamp out four cake layers.

② Place a piece of parchment or wax paper on the plate where you will build the cake. I try to use a plate that is only slightly bigger than the cake itself, because I never have much free space in the freezer. The cake will be frozen in Step 7. Place the cake ring over the parchment, and line the ring with the circle of acetate.

Continued

③ **BOTTOM LAYER:** Gently drop in a circle cut from the Whole Wheat Chocolate Chip Cake. (Reserve the smoothest circle for the top layer of the cake.) Don't worry if it gets damaged when you drop it in; this layer will be covered. If it doesn't land perfectly, just smoosh it into the ring. Spread a fourth (about ¼ cup) of the Coffee Frosting over the cake. Spread a third (about ⅔ cup) of the Passionfruit Curd over the frosting as evenly as you can manage. Sprinkle about ⅓ cup of the Barley Chocolate Crumbs over the curd.

④ **SECOND LAYER:** Repeat Step 3.

⑤ **THIRD LAYER:** Repeat Step 3.

⑥ **TOP LAYER:** Gently place the last layer of cake. As evenly as possible, spread remaining Coffee Frosting over the cake. Sprinkle chocolate chips over the top.

⑦ Cover with plastic wrap. Freeze cake overnight or at least 8 hours. At least 3 hours before you are ready to serve the cake, pull it out of the freezer and pop it out of the ring using your fingers and thumbs to press it out from the bottom. Gently peel off the acetate ring, and transfer the cake to a serving platter or cake stand. Let it defrost in the refrigerator for a minimum of 3 hours. Before serving, sprinkle about a quarter cup of Barley Chocolate Crumbs around the cake base.

WHOLE-WHEAT CHOCOLATE CHIP CAKE

Even if you don't plan to build the Jupiter Cake, this sheet cake is well worth making. With its excess of both vanilla and chocolate, it is delicious by itself and even better with a cup of coffee. The sticky caramelized exterior is reminiscent of the buttery top of pineapple upside-down cake.

If you plan to make the Jupiter Cake, you can make these cake layers up to a month in advance to freeze or 5 days ahead to refrigerate. The most space-saving method is to go ahead and cut out the cake circles (see page 117), stack them between wax paper and wrap the stacked and separated layers tightly in plastic wrap. Add an outer layer of foil protection if you plan to freeze.

YIELD: One ¼-sheet cake, or four 6-inch circles for a layer cake

INGREDIENTS:

1½ c. (120g) whole-wheat pastry flour

1 tsp. (5g) baking powder

1 tsp. (4g) salt

1 stick (8 tbsp./113g) unsalted butter, between 65 and 70 degrees Fahrenheit

Cooking spray or lard for greasing pans

1½ c. (240g) coconut sugar or granulated sugar

3 large eggs (150g)

½ c. (110g) buttermilk (see recipe on page 124), yogurt, or kefir

½ c. (108g) coconut oil, grapeseed oil, or light-flavored olive oil

1 tbsp. (12g) vanilla extract

¾ c. (128g) mini chocolate chips

INSTRUCTIONS:

① Preheat oven to 350 degrees Fahrenheit (177 degrees Celsius).

② In a food processor or mixing bowl, sift together flour, baking powder, and salt.

③ Line a quarter-sheet baking pan (also called a jelly roll pan) with parchment paper or silicone mat. Or grease lightly with cooking spray or lard, then dust lightly with flour.

④ Combine butter and sugar in the bowl of a stand mixer fitted with paddle attachment, or use a hand mixer. Cream butter and sugar on medium-high speed for at least 3 minutes, intermittently scraping down the sides of the bowl with a spatula. Add eggs and mix on medium-high for 2 to 3 minutes. Scrape down sides.

(5) With mixer on low speed, slowly stream in buttermilk, oil, and vanilla. Increase speed to medium-high and paddle for at least 6 minutes, scraping down sides occasionally. The mixture should be completely homogenous and about twice the size of the fluffy butter-sugar mixture. Don't rush this process. You're forcing liquid into an already fatty mixture that doesn't want to make room for the liquid. This is the secret to the cake's lusciousness.

(6) Scrape down sides of the bowl. With mixer running on lowest speed, add sifted flour mixture. Mix just until batter comes together and any remnants of dry ingredients disappear, about 45 to 60 seconds. Scrape down sides of bowl. If you see any dry ingredients, mix again briefly to incorporate.

(7) Using your largest spatula, spread batter in an even layer in prepared pan. Give pan a tap on the countertop to further even out the layer. Try not to destroy the fluffiness you've worked so hard to build. Sprinkle chocolate chips evenly over top.

(8) Bake cake 22 to 25 minutes. It should puff to double its size, but will remain buttery and dense. At 22 minutes, gently poke the cake close to an edge. It should bounce back slightly, and the center should no longer jiggle. Bake for 3 to 5 minutes more if cake doesn't pass these tests.

(9) Remove cake from oven and cool (in the pan) on a wire rack, or in a pinch, in the fridge or freezer set on trivets. Place a piece of parchment paper at least as big as the cake on a counter. When cake has cooled slightly, invert pan in one firm and decisive motion onto parchment paper. At this point, you can serve cake immediately or follow Step 1 on page 117 for cutting out layers for the Jupiter Cake.

COFFEE FROSTING

The only part of the original *Momofuku Milk Bar* recipe I really did not like was the coffee frosting. I've changed the recipe to make it lighter. If you don't have espresso powder on hand, omit it and the milk; in Step 4, incorporate strong, chilled, brewed coffee instead of milk.

YIELD: 1 cup (200 grams), enough to fill the Jupiter Cake on page 117

INGREDIENTS:

2 c. (240g) powdered sugar

¼ tsp. (1g) salt

6 to 8 tbsp. (85 to 113g) unsalted butter, cut into pats, at room temperature

2 tsp. (8g) vanilla extract

2 tsp. (2g) instant espresso or coffee powder

½ c. (57g) whole milk, at room temperature

INSTRUCTIONS:

(1) In a mixing bowl, whisk together powdered sugar and salt.

(2) In a separate mixing bowl with a hand mixer or whisk, or in the bowl of a stand mixer with paddle attachment, beat butter with vanilla and espresso powder for a few minutes on medium-high speed, until creamy. (If at any point, mixture begins to look oily or as if the butter is melting, stop immediately, and chill bowl in refrigerator for 10 minutes.)

(3) Reduce to medium speed, and incorporate dry ingredients.

Reduce to low speed, and add milk a little at a time, until desired consistency is reached. Stop as needed to scrape down sides of bowl.

Continued

Jupiter Cake . . . *continued*

PASSIONFRUIT OR ORANGE CURD

The sweet-tangy flavor of passionfruit is unparalleled, but it is hard to find unless you live in a tropical area or have access to a Latin grocery store. Passionfruit purée is also available via Amazon.com. Luckily, you can substitute orange juice for passionfruit juice with wonderful results, especially because orange juice works so well with whole wheat. This is one recipe in which I prefer to use granulated white sugar to avoid overpowering the fruit with any flavor other than sweet.

This curd could easily replace the curd in a traditional lemon bar or become the filling of a fully baked whole-grain pie crust, such as the one on page 51.

YIELD: 2 cups (480 grams) curd, enough to fill the Jupiter Cake on page 117

INGREDIENTS:

2 large eggs (100g)

½ c. granulated sugar (110g)

¾ c. (170g) passionfruit juice or purée (or orange juice)

2 tbsp. (28g) lemon juice

1½ sticks (12 tbsp./169g) unsalted butter, very cold, cut into tablespoon pats

¼ tsp. (1g) salt

INSTRUCTIONS:

① In a stainless-steel bowl, whisk together eggs, sugar, and fruit juice until well-combined. Set bowl over a pan of gently simmering water. Cook for 2 minutes, stirring and scraping the sides and bottom of pan constantly with a spatula.

② Begin adding butter a pat at a time, stirring continuously. Add each additional pat of butter after previous one is fully incorporated. This process will take several minutes.

③ Stir in salt and continue cooking while stirring and scraping for 5 to 10 minutes more. The curd will thicken and lighten in color. Do not allow it to approach a boil. When curd coats spatula without much dripping and you can draw your finger through it to leave a path, immediately remove bowl from heat. If you like to use a thermometer to judge doneness, it should be about 165 degrees Fahrenheit (75 degrees Celsius). Eggs will begin to scramble as it gets hotter.

④ To ensure a silky texture and strain out any bits of scrambled egg, press curd through a fine-mesh sieve set over a nonreactive bowl. If not using curd immediately, cover with plastic wrap once curd has cooled completely. Press plastic onto surface of curd to prevent it forming a skin. Most recipes require curd to be well-chilled, at least an hour in the refrigerator. It will keep for up to 2 weeks in the refrigerator. Freezing fruit curd is not recommended.

PASSIONFRUIT TART

You can also use this curd to make a tangy tart. Double the curd recipe above, and chill the curd overnight. On the same day of curd-making, follow the procedure for making the Whole-Wheat Pie Crust on page 51, substituting ⅓ cup of finely chopped macadamia nuts—or another favorite nut—for ⅓ cup of the flour. Chill a pie pan lined with this crust overnight in freezer.

The next day, bake the crust following the instructions for Blind Baking on page 53. Let crust cool, fill it with the chilled curd, and smooth the top. Chill tart for at least an hour before serving.

BARLEY CHOCOLATE CRUMBS

Most of Milk Bar's treats involve some crumbly, crunchy bits. All are delicious on their own as a little treat, or sprinkled over yogurt, oatmeal, or ice cream. This intensely dark crumble is no exception. The flour here is not essential for rise, so you can use any kind of flour you like.

YIELD: About 2½ cups (350 grams), enough to use in the Jupiter Cake on page 117 and still have some left for snacking. They'll stay fresh if kept in an airtight container at room temperature for up to a week or at least a month in the freezer.

INGREDIENTS:

⅔ c. (62g) barley flour or other whole-grain flour

½ c. (80g) coconut sugar or granulated sugar

⅔ c. (55g) dark cocoa powder

1 tsp. (4g) kosher salt

6 tbsp. (85g) unsalted butter, melted

INSTRUCTIONS:

① Preheat oven to 300 degrees Fahrenheit (149 degrees Celsius). Line a baking sheet with parchment paper or silicone mat.

② Combine flour, sugar, cocoa powder, and salt in bowl of a stand mixer fitted with paddle. Beat on low speed until well-mixed.

③ With mixer running, add butter slowly in a stream. Turn off mixer when small clusters begin to form.

④ Spread clusters on baking pan. Bake for 20 minutes, breaking them up a few times while baking. The crumbs will be slightly moist when you remove them from oven and harden as they cool.

THINGS TO EAT WITH BREAD

Whole-grain breads have much more flavor than white breads, but that doesn't mean they don't like some company from time to time. As good as homemade whole-grain breads can be, you can make them even better using homemade spreads and other toppings made with fresh, whole ingredients that boost both flavor and nutrition.

For ideas about pairing specific grains with specific flavors, see the Whole Grains Glossary on page 13. Besides fresh flavors, making your own bread *and* butter has the added benefit of making you feel a great sense of accomplishment.

FABULOUS HOMEMADE BUTTER
(AND REAL BUTTERMILK)

If there's nothing like freshly baked bread, there's *really* nothing like fresh bread with creamy, homemade butter. You may use light or heavy cream, or a mixture. You can make any amount, because extra butter freezes well. During the process, you will also get buttermilk that is fresher tasting than what you'll find in the grocery store.

To salt or not is up to you. Unsalted butter is more versatile for cooking, but salted butter made from homemade cultured cream is a treat.

It's hardly worth making your own butter if you don't have good cream. For me, this means organic, raw, or at least not ultrapasteurized cream. Good stuff like this is become increasingly available—thank goodness.

SWEET CREAM BUTTER

Sweet cream butter—made from unripened, or "sweet," cream—is the easiest butter you can make. Simply agitate cream until the butterfat globules in it stick together enough to separate out from the buttermilk. This recipe suggests using a food processor, but if you don't have one you can go really low-tech and shake the cream in a canning jar.

YIELD: You can start with any amount of cream. 1 quart yields about 1 pound (454g) of butter, though amounts vary depending on butterfat content of cream.

INGREDIENT:

1 qt. (907g) very cold cream

INSTRUCTIONS:

① Chill cream in refrigerator for at least an hour. While you're at it, put the following items in the fridge too: the bowl of a food processor fitted with its blade; a mesh strainer; a spatula, wooden spoon or potato masher; and a mixing bowl. Also adjust your kitchen's temperature down a few notches if it's especially warm. Cold is key for best flavor. (According to milk expert Anne Mendelson, every few degrees of temperature above 45 or 50 degrees Fahrenheit, 7 to 10 degrees Celsius, mean some loss of flavor compounds.)

② Prepare a bowl of ice water and set it aside.

③ Process cream on high speed. You'll begin to see it thicken into whipped cream. As you pass the stage of whipped cream, the white liquid will begin to yellow and become gritty. At this stage, begin pulsing the machine. Stop pulsing when you see an obvious separation of solid globs of butter from liquid buttermilk.

④ Pour contents through a fine-mesh strainer set over a bowl. Pour strained buttermilk into a jar. Refrigerate or freeze to use in buttermilk recipes, though note that it will not have the flavor of cultured buttermilk. (For that, see page 126.)

⑤ Dump butter globs into mixing bowl. Pour 2 cups strained ice water into the bowl. Using a spatula, wooden spoon, or potato masher, smoosh butter clumps together into a cohesive mass, then pour off the water, which will now be cloudy from pressing out more buttermilk.

Press butter against sides of bowl over and over, expelling as much buttermilk as you can. The butter will become smoother and shinier. At this last stage, you may incorporate a teaspoon or more of salt if you'd like salted butter. When you don't see any more buttermilk coming out, refrigerate butter in a sealed container to prevent it from absorbing other flavors. Eat fresh butter within about 5 days, or freeze it to maintain best flavor.

Continued

CULTURED (ALSO KNOWN AS THE BEST) BUTTER

Cultured butter is often sold as European-style butter. What this means is that before churning, the cream was cultured, ripened, fermented, or soured. Whatever you want to call the process, it means things got tangy. Most dairy the world over has been consumed this way. Both the butter and buttermilk are more flavorful than if using sweet cream.

To make raw (unpasteurized) cream sour or ripe, all you have to do is leave it alone at room temperature for a day or two. It contains the natural bacteria that will sour, and consequently flavor, it. Once it has become sour, you can use it in the instructions here to make cultured butter. It will come, or separate into butterfat and buttermilk, much faster than sweet cream.

If you do not have access to raw cream from a farm that you absolutely know and trust to be clean and safe, your best option is to purchase high-quality pasteurized cream and ferment it yourself by adding a starter that contains live cultures. You could use buttermilk from a previous batch of butter-making, or buttermilk, crème fraîche, sour cream, or yogurt from a package whose label indicates that it contains live cultures. My favorite-flavored cultured butter comes from using a powdered bacterial starter for making crème fraîche that I buy from New England Cheesemaking Supply (cheesemaking.com).

YIELD: About 1 pound (454 grams) of butter, though amounts vary depending on butterfat content of cream

INGREDIENTS:

1 qt. (907g) very cold cream

¼ c. (57g) liquid cultured dairy containing live cultures, such as buttermilk, crème fraîche, sour cream, or yogurt; or 1 packet powdered crème fraîche starter

INSTRUCTIONS:

① In a saucepan, heat cream to 86 degrees Fahrenheit (30 degrees Celsius). Stir in the liquid cultured dairy. Or sprinkle powdered starter evenly over cream, and stir it in gently. Put a lid on the pot and set it aside.

② Allow cream to ripen for 16 to 24 hours if using buttermilk, crème fraîche, sour cream, or yogurt as a starter, or for 12 hours if using powdered crème fraîche starter. Once cream is thick and smells tangy, chill in refrigerator overnight.

③ Follow instructions on page 124 to churn the cultured cream into cultured butter and cultured buttermilk (instead of sweet cream and sweet buttermilk).

GARLIC AND BASIL INFUSED OLIVE OIL

This oil forms the basis of the simple but flavorful tomato sauce featured in Andrew Carmellini's *Urban Italian*—a top-ten cookbook in our house. Carmellini strains everything out of the oil and pours it into a bunch of tomatoes (5 pounds) simmering with a teaspoon of salt to make his signature sauce. It's wonderful that way, but we prefer to leave the infusion ingredients in and serve the oil by itself as a dip. Puréeing the whole mixture to use as a condiment is also excellent.

YIELD: About 1¼ cups (283 grams) infused oil

INGREDIENTS:

1 head (57g) garlic

1¼ c. (284g) extra-virgin olive oil

1 large handful basil leaves, rinsed and patted dry

1 tsp. (2g) red pepper flakes

INSTRUCTIONS:

① Cut the top off the garlic head so most of the skin stays on but the tops of the cloves are exposed.

② Combine garlic, oil, basil, and pepper flakes in a small saucepan over medium heat and bring to a simmer. As soon as you hear the basil crack (yes, you'll hear it), take the mixture off heat and reserve.

③ At this point, you can store the infused oil in the refrigerator, where it will solidify. If you like, you may strain the solids out or purée the oil with its solids before refrigerating.

④ Use the solidified infused oil by the spoonful in sautés. To serve again as a dip, let it come to room temperature first.

OLIVE TAPENADE

Use any olives that you find tasty. Try buttery, green castelvetrano; chewy, brownish nicoise; salty, purple kalamata; and bitter, black Moroccan olives. The flavor of olive oil will come through in this recipe—use a good one. In a recent taste test I conducted, Georgia Olive Farms' cold-pressed, extra-virgin olive oil (georgiaolivefarms.com) was the unanimous winner over eight other American-grown oils.

Tapenade is an excellent vehicle for flavor experimentation. Feel free to add small amounts of capers, roasted nuts, fresh figs, sun-dried tomatoes, anchovies, and nearly any combination of fresh herbs.

YIELD: 1 to 2 cups (227 to 454 grams)

INGREDIENTS:

1 c. (170g) pitted olives

1 clove (6g) garlic

2 tsp. (9g) lemon juice

¼ to ½ c. (57 to 113g) extra-virgin olive oil

INSTRUCTIONS:

① In a food processor, chop up pitted olives, garlic, and lemon juice, plus any optional add-ins.

② While machine is running, pour in olive oil slowly in a stream, until a chunky paste is formed. (Continue processing if you'd rather have a smooth spread.) Serve on toasted crostini as an appetizer, in a sandwich as a condiment, or tossed with pasta as a sauce.

CARAMELIZED ONIONS, SHALLOTS, LEEKS, or FENNEL

Some crops store energy as starch. The energy the onion family runs on, however, is sugar. Slowly cooking these alliums releases and transforms all those sugars into something new and altogether magnificent. Everyone's favorite food scientist, Harold McGee (CuriousCook.com), explains that caramelization is the name given to "a remarkable cascade of chemical creation" that occurs when any sugar is heated to the point that its molecules begin to break apart, forming hundreds of new and different flavor compounds.

Because caramelizing is the work of a patient cook, you may maximize your time investment by preparing extras, which will freeze well for up to 6 months. Let the remarkable cascade begin!

YIELD: About 1 cup, packed full

INGREDIENTS:

2 tbsp. (28g) olive oil

1 lb. (454g) total of any of the following: onions, shallots, leeks (white and pale green parts only), and/or fennel (white bulbs only), chopped

2 tsp. (8g) salt

2 tsp. (10g) sherry vinegar or apple cider vinegar

4 tsp. (10g) sherry or white wine (sherry will be sweeter)

4 tsp. (20g) brown sugar or honey

4 sprigs (4g) fresh thyme

Freshly ground pepper, to taste

Water, as needed

INSTRUCTIONS:

① Heat oil in a heavy-bottomed skillet or deep pan over medium-low heat. Sauté onions/shallots/leeks/fennel for 2 minutes, then sprinkle with salt and sauté another 5 minutes, or until soft. Reduce heat to low if necessary to prevent browning too quickly.

② Add remaining ingredients except water, and sauté another 20 minutes, stirring occasionally. Add water as needed to prevent sticking and burning, about a tablespoon at a time. Remove sprigs of thyme before serving on bread.

MAPLE BUTTER

If yours is among the lucky palates that have enjoyed real maple syrup, you probably don't need convincing to go out and get some. Not only is it richer and more nuanced than the fake stuff made of high-fructose corn syrup, but indulging in it is a great way to participate in the revival of regional specialties.

Pure maple syrup flavor ranges from light and delicate (Grade A Light and Medium Amber) to complex and robust (Grade A Dark Amber, Grade B). Find producers near you at farmers markets or through the state-by-state listings at Local Harvest (localharvest.org).

As soon as you get your hands on some fresh maple syrup, try turning a little bit into a wonderful spread for biscuits or toasted homemade bread. Creamy maple butter has a peanut-buttery consistency along with maple syrup's deep, nourishing flavors. Maple pairs well with any grain, and helps balance strong flavors like buckwheat.

YIELD: Makes about 1½ cups (340 grams)

INGREDIENTS:

1 c. (227g) pure maple syrup

¾ c. (170g) butter, softened

INSTRUCTIONS:

① Heat maple syrup in a heavy-bottomed pan until it foams. This usually takes about 10 minutes. If you have a thermometer, you can check the temperature, which should be about 240 degrees Fahrenheit (116 degrees Celsius). This is often called the "softball stage."

② Stir in butter and pour mixture into a mixing bowl or the bowl of a stand mixer. With a hand mixer or stand mixer fitted with the paddle attachment, beat mixture until it's thick and creamy. This also takes about 10 minutes.

③ Pour maple butter into a glass jar with a lid and refrigerate. Serve on biscuits, cornbread, rolls, and toast.

MIXED TOMATO JAM

With notes both sweet and tart, tomatoes are a perfect fruit for jamming. This jam is best if you use a variety of heirloom tomatoes, and it's perfectly fine to use the less-expensive tomatoes known as "seconds" or "canners"—just cut out the bad spots that no one will see.

YIELD: About 2 pints (454 grams) jam, depending on juiciness of tomatoes and how long you cook them down.

INGREDIENTS:

2 lb. (907g) ripe tomatoes of any type

⅔ c. (140g) palm sugar or granulated sugar

Juice and zest of one medium lime (or 2 tbsp./28g bottled lime juice plus 1 tbsp./3g dried lime peel)

2 tsp. (8g) salt

2 tsp. (4g) ground ginger (or a 1-inch piece of fresh ginger, peeled)

2 tsp. (4g) ground coriander (or 2 tsp. coriander seeds)

1 tsp. (2g) ground cinnamon (or a 3-inch stick)

½ tsp. (1g) ground star anise (or 1 whole star anise)

KITCHEN TIP: If you prefer to use whole spices, put slices of fresh ginger, coriander seeds, cinnamon stick, and star anise in a muslin spice/tea bag, then remove the bag when the jam is finished.

INSTRUCTIONS:

① Core tomatoes and chop roughly. If you're short on time, just cut them in half. If using cherry, grape, or pear tomatoes, don't bother cutting them at all. There's no need to remove the seedy pulp, but you can if you don't like tomato seeds.

② Add all ingredients to a deep, heavy-bottomed pot. Bring to a simmer over medium heat, stirring occasionally, until mixture begins to thicken. This can take up to an hour. If you need to speed things up, turn up the heat, but stand by to watch and stir. If you need to slow things down, turn it down. (If you happen to be using rock-hard palm sugar, just keep stirring until it melts.)

③ When most of the watery tomato juice is cooked out, reduce heat to low and continue to simmer, stirring frequently, until mixture is nice and jammy, keeping in mind that it will set up even more as it cools.

④ Allow jam to cool. Fish out any whole spices. Cover and store in the refrigerator where it'll easily last a week or more.

THINGS TO DO WITH LEFTOVER BREAD

It's a shame to let good bread go bad. If we're talking about homemade bread, it's an even bigger tragedy. Luckily, bread never really goes bad unless you let it mold, and you can easily save it from the brink by removing or restoring moisture. With good storage techniques (see page 148), your freshly baked breads will last several days. When that time is up, you can turn staling bread into infinitely useful croutons and breadcrumbs. Most of the recipes in this chapter begin with homemade croutons.

CROUTONS MANY WAYS

Croutons are useful for more than a Caesar salad. Pulverize them into breadcrumbs to thicken a soup, pan-fry them into the start of a filling meal, stuff them into a turkey, or soak them in custard for dessert.

You can make croutons out of any bread, but consider the end use. Are the flavors in your stale bread the same flavors you want in your gratin topping? Will the tang of sourdough be a nice counterpoint to the chocolate in your dessert? Would you enjoy rye bread in that soup?

The best way I've found to make use of stale bread is to save unseasoned croutons from neutral-flavored breads and sweet breads, and seasoned croutons from savory breads. Any of these three types of stored croutons can be turned into fine or coarse breadcrumbs in a jiffy (see page 135).

UNSEASONED CROUTONS

① Preheat oven to 375 degrees Fahrenheit (190 degrees Celsius).

② Cut or tear any amount of leftover bread into roughly 1-inch chunks. Place them one layer deep on a baking sheet.

③ Bake until crispy, thoroughly dry, and toasted on all sides, anywhere from 20 minutes to an hour, depending on the moisture left in your bread. Toss them around a few times during cooking to help toast all sides evenly.

SEASONED CROUTONS

Before embarking on Step 1 above, toss cubes of bread in enough dry herbs to coat evenly. You may prefer not to add salt—that way you can use them for cooking later without worrying that they'll add too much salt to a dish. Do not add any oil, cheese, or fresh garlic if you plan to store the croutons for a while, but feel free to add any flavors you like if you'll use them right away.

PAN-FRIED CROUTONS

Pan frying *semidry* bread is the best way to achieve a crouton that is perfectly crispy on the outside yet chewy on the inside. You can use bread that has already dried out completely, but it won't be as chewy inside.

1 Preheat a wide skillet over medium-high for a few minutes. Carefully pour in Garlic and Basil Infused Oil (recipe on page 127) or plain olive oil until it reaches about a quarter of an inch deep.

2 Add cubed bread, turning carefully to coat all sides with oil.

3 Fry bread about 10 to 15 minutes, turning cubes until all sides are golden-brown.

4 Transfer to towel to drain and cool. Sprinkle with salt while hot.

GRILLED CROUTONS

Instead of cubing leftover bread, grill whole slices into extra-large croutons to accompany a breakfast of scrambled eggs, an appetizer of tapenade (recipe on page 128), or a lunch salad.

1 Preheat grill or grill pan to medium-high.

2 Brush both sides of whole slices of bread with Garlic and Basil Infused Oil (recipe on page 127). Or rub a raw garlic clove all over both sides of each slice, then brush with olive oil.

3 Grill each side until well-toasted, about 10 minutes total.

BREADCRUMBS

Breadcrumbs are a pantry staple around the world and end up in a surprising array of recipes. At Jim Lahey's Sullivan Street Bakery in New York, unseasoned breadcrumbs are an essential ingredient in a chocolate torte, where they add body. If you've ever had tomato gazpacho that didn't taste like salsa, the unseen difference was probably breadcrumbs.

1 To make and store breadcrumbs successfully, the bread must be completely dry. If in doubt, spread your bread cubes on a baking sheet and toast it at 375 degrees Fahrenheit (190 degrees Celsius) until you're sure.

2 Pour croutons, seasoned or unseasoned, into a food processor until it is no more than halfway full. Push the pulse button several times, until the breadcrumbs achieve your desired consistency. Warning: This process is shockingly loud! (Alternately, crush the bread with a rolling pin. Warning: This process is shockingly messy.)

3 Store breadcrumbs in an airtight container.

HIGH SUMMER PANZANELLA

This bread salad is a wonderful way to use late-summer bounty. Substitute other vegetables as necessary to use whatever is abundant. Panzanella is a perfect vehicle for whole-grain croutons with strong flavors such as amaranth, buckwheat, and teff.

YIELD: 6 servings

INGREDIENTS:

Grated zest and juice of 1 medium lemon

3 tsp. (12g) salt, divided

4 tbsp. (56g) extra virgin olive oil, divided

½ lb. (about 4 leaves or 227g) kale, preferably 'Lacinato' or dinosaur kale

½ lb. (about 4 leaves or 227g) rainbow Swiss chard

1 medium zucchini (284g) or 2 handfuls baby zucchini, chopped into bite-sized pieces

1 medium yellow squash (284g) or 2 handfuls baby squash, chopped into bite-sized pieces

8 whole cippolini onions (400g), with outer skin removed (or 2 large yellow onions, peeled and cut into chunks)

1 large or 2 small sweet peppers (160g), chopped into bite-sized pieces, seeds and stems removed

1 c. (227g) sweet corn kernels (from 2 medium ears)

2 c. Pan-Fried Croutons (page 135)

½ c. (227g) Roasted Tomato Vinaigrette (recipe follows)

1 handful fresh basil leaves, whole or torn into smaller pieces

1 oz. (28g) Parmesan or Grana Padano cheese

INSTRUCTIONS:

① Add lemon zest and juice to a large mixing bowl. Whisk in a teaspoon of salt and 2 tablespoons olive oil.

② Trim fibrous stalks from kale and chard by slicing leaves down the center on either side of stalk. Chop stalks into ½-inch pieces. Set aside. Stack several strips of greens on top of each other and roll them into a bundle. Slice the bundle into thin strips, or chiffonades. Continue with remaining greens. Toss greens in lemon juice-oil mixture. Cover and refrigerate at least an hour or overnight. (At this point, you have a tasty salad on its own—as long as you let it marinate for a while.)

③ Preheat oven to 350 degrees Fahrenheit (175 degrees Celsius). Toss zucchini, squash, onions, peppers, and reserved kale and chard stalks with 2 teaspoons salt and 2 tablespoons oil. Roast vegetables in a single layer in a baking pan for 20 minutes or until soft. Add corn, stir, and roast another 20 minutes. At this point, you can build the salad or chill vegetables first for a cold salad. I prefer everything chilled except the cheese. (Always let cheese come to room temperature before serving.)

④ In a large bowl, toss marinated greens, roasted vegetables, and croutons with vinaigrette. To serve, shave several large pieces of Parmesan onto each salad and sprinkle with basil.

ROASTED TOMATO VINAIGRETTE

This chunky vinaigrette is sweet, tart, and versatile and freezes well for months. It's great hot or cold, spread on toast, or tossed with salad or pasta. For best flavor, use a mixture of tomato varieties.

YIELD: 2 cups (535 grams)

INGREDIENTS FOR ROASTED TOMATOES:

2 tbsp. (28g) extra virgin olive oil

2 tbsp. (28g) balsamic vinegar

½ tsp. (2g) minced fresh garlic

½ tsp. (2g) salt

A few twists (2g) freshly ground pepper

1 lb. (454g) ripe tomatoes

½ medium sweet pepper (60g), seeds, stem, and ribs removed, cut into large chunks

½ medium red onion (about ½ cup or 60g), peeled and quartered

INGREDIENTS FOR VINAIGRETTE:

2 tbsp. (28g) balsamic vinegar

½ tsp. (2g) minced fresh garlic

2 dashes vinegary hot sauce, such as Tabasco

1 handful fresh basil leaves

1 sprig fresh thyme (1 tsp./3g leaves)

¼ c. (56g) extra virgin olive oil

INSTRUCTIONS:

① Preheat oven to 325 degrees Fahrenheit (165 degrees Celsius). In a baking dish, whisk together 2 tablespoons olive oil, 2 tablespoons balsamic vinegar, ½ teaspoon garlic, salt, and pepper.

② Cut large tomatoes in half. Leave cherry and pear tomatoes whole. Toss tomatoes, sweet pepper, and onion in baking dish with seasoned oil-vinegar blend from Step 1. Roast 30 minutes. Tomato and pepper skins will wrinkle. When mixture is cool, remove skins by hand or by passing ingredients through a food mill.

③ Add roasted mixture, including juices, to food processor or blender. Add remaining vinegar and garlic, plus hot sauce, basil, and thyme. Pulse a few times for chunky dressing, or purée for smooth dressing. Add remaining oil in a stream with processor/blender running. Pour into a lidded container and refrigerate. For refrigerator storage, I like to use a salad dressing jar designed to re-emulsify dressing at each time of use, such as the Chef'n Emulstir (online at chefn.com), which is one of the few models on the market that actually has a lid to cover the pour spout.

FRENCH SHALLOT SOUP

This version of the classic French onion soup is easy to put together. It takes a long time, but most is hands-off time. For the best flavor, don't rush the soup and don't skip the wine and cognac. I used to make French onion soup with painstakingly produced rich beef bone stock. That version is incredible, but using plain water is simpler and is a nice way to let the shallot flavor shine above all. Hearty breads with an open crumb, such as whole-grain baguettes, are ideal for this recipe.

YIELD: 4 servings

INGREDIENTS:

1 c. caramelized shallots or onions (recipe on page 129)

2 tsp. (9g) unsalted butter

1 qt. (907g) water

1 c. (227g) dry red or white wine

1 to 2 tsp. (5 to 10g) Cognac for each bowl of soup

4 large or 8 small slices stale bread

4 oz. (114g) Gruyère cheese, grated or sliced

INSTRUCTIONS:

① Melt butter over medium-low heat in a deep pan, stockpot, or Dutch oven. Add caramelized shallots and stir to warm through. Add water and wine. Simmer for at least 20 minutes and up to 40 minutes. Near the end of cooking time, preheat oven broiler.

② Divide soup into four ovenproof bowls, and stir 1 to 2 teaspoons Cognac into each bowl. Gently float a slice of bread in each, then add the cheese atop the bread. Broil until golden and bubbly, about 3 to 5 minutes. Be sure to watch carefully to prevent burning.

OYSTER, SAUSAGE, AND APPLE DRESSING

This has been my favorite family Thanksgiving dish for years—ever since my dad decided to go out on a limb with canned smoked oysters from the back of the pantry. Even though it's not the way my dad does it, you might try shucking live oysters if a grocery store near you carries them or can special order them. (Expect to pay about a dollar per oyster.) It's fun. You can eat a few while you're at it. The first Thanksgiving likely included freshly shucked oysters. Need any other excuses to give it a go?

Dressing-making time is the perfect time to use up stale bread studded with herbs, cheese, olives, or other savory add-ins. Baked stuffing freezes well if wrapped tightly. Consider making this ahead of time to reduce Thanksgiving Day prep.

YIELD: 8 to 10 servings, as a side

INGREDIENTS:

5 oz. (about 4 thick-cut strips or 140g) bacon

2 small or 1 large onion (170g)

5 ribs (170g) celery

2 tart apples (300g), such as Braeburn, Granny Smith, or Northern Spy, seeded and diced, with peels on

1 c. (227g) corn kernels (from about 2 medium ears)

1 tsp. (4g) salt

Several twists freshly ground pepper

15 leaves fresh or dried sage

3 sprigs fresh thyme (or 1 tbsp. or 3g dried)

2 sprigs fresh oregano (or 2 tsp. or 2g dried)

Small handful fresh basil (or 1 basil ice cube)

Small handful fresh parsley (or 1 parsley ice cube)

Continued

8 oz. (227g) sweet Italian sausage

1 dozen live oysters (or one 4-oz. can)

Hot sauce, to taste

2 large eggs (100g), beaten

2 c. (454g) seafood, vegetable, or mushroom stock

Approximately 4 c. (210g) Seasoned or Unseasoned Croutons (recipe on page 134)

4 c. cornbread, crumbled into chunks (recipe on page 38)

KITCHEN TIP: Herb ice cubes are great for use in fall and winter. When herbs are in season, blend chopped herbs with olive oil or water and freeze in ice cube trays. When frozen, pop them out into a storage container.

INSTRUCTIONS:

① Preheat oven to 350 degrees Fahrenheit (175 degrees Celsius).

② Fry bacon over medium-high heat in your widest, deepest skillet. When it's cooked through, transfer to towel to drain. Dice bacon into whatever size pieces you'd like to bite into and set aside.

③ Sauté onion, celery, apple, and corn in bacon grease until soft, about 5 minutes. Stir in salt, pepper, and herbs.

④ In the same pan, cook sausage until heated through. Remove from heat and chop into bite-sized pieces.

⑤ To shuck oysters, see right. Chop oysters into two to three pieces each. Toss them along with the nutritious and delicious liquid in the shells known as *oyster liquor* into your biggest mixing bowl.

⑥ Add croutons, cornbread, bacon, sautéed vegetables, sausage, hot sauce, and beaten eggs. (Much of the cornbread will crumble even further.) Add stock, a little bit at a time, tossing to coat evenly, until the mixture is uniformly moist. You may not use all of the stock.

⑦ Press mixture into a greased 9-by-13-inch baking pan. Bake on your oven's middle rack for 35 minutes or until the top begins to brown yet the interior is still somewhat moist. For a crunchy topping, broil the stuffing for up to 5 minutes with the oven door slightly ajar. Serve warm.

HOW TO SHUCK AN OYSTER

It's easy to hurt yourself shucking oysters. Some professional shuckers wear chain-mail gloves, but that's not necessary if you go slow. You can find oyster knives at kitchen stores. Pick something solid and durable rather than attractive. It should have a steel blade and slip-resistant handle.

INSTRUCTIONS:

① Choose oysters that are tightly closed. If an oyster is open slightly, tap it. If it doesn't close, toss it out.

② Refrigerate oysters until ready to use. Set them in a single layer in a deep dish, with the cup sides (whichever sides protrude most) down. Cover them with a damp towel. They can remain this way for 1 day.

③ With a clean brush, scrub both sides of oyster shell under running water to remove debris.

④ Using a towel set on a countertop, hold the oyster securely in place, with its cup side down and the hinge pointing toward you. Insert the tip of the knife into the middle of the hinge. Point the blade down slightly, toward the countertop. While firmly pressing the knife into the hinge, twist the blade to the right and back and forth. Continue twisting while applying pressure until the hinge pops. This may feel awkward at first, but once you get an oyster to pop open, you'll have a sense of how much pressure to use on the next one.

⑤ Drag the knife around the entire oyster where the halves meet. Work slowly and gently to pry the halves apart.

⑥ When the two halves have split, you need to disconnect the oyster from the shell. Scrape the blade along the underside of the top shell, above the oyster, until you have clipped the connecting muscle. The top shell can now be discarded. Now do the same thing underneath the oyster, attempting to retain the oyster liquor in the cup. Carefully fish out any bits of shell or grit.

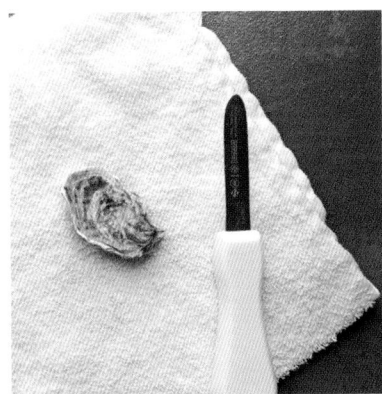

Pick a solid oyster knife with a slip-resistant handle.

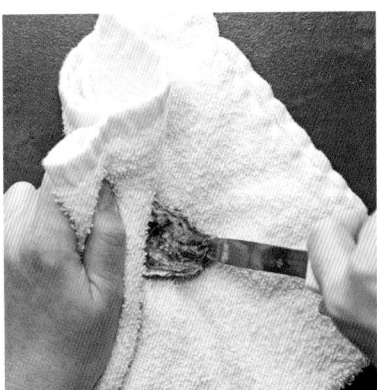

Insert the tip of the knife into the middle of the hinge.

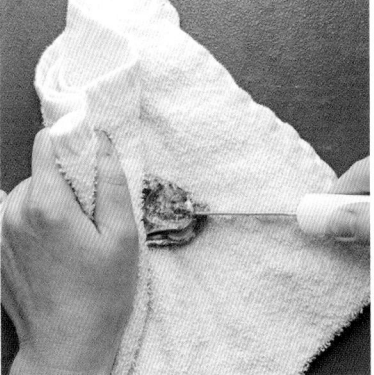

Twist until the hinge pops.

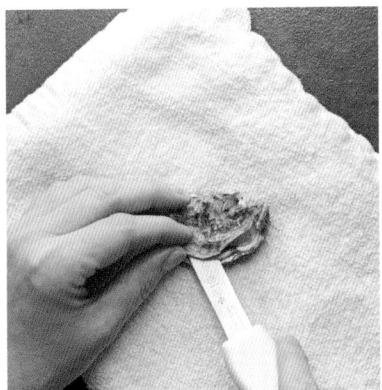

Cut the top muscle.

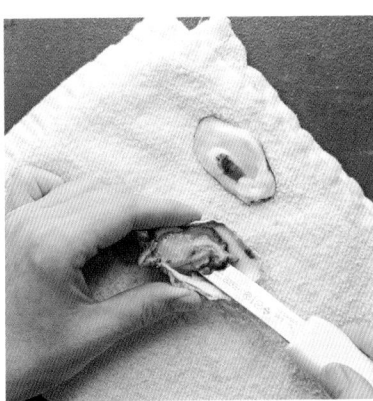

Cut the bottom muscle.

BUTTERNUT SQUASH GRATIN

Sweet, tender butternut squash pairs well with nutty-flavored breadcrumbs from whole-grain breads. This dish can be prepped in advance and frozen for an easy dinner on a busy night.

YIELD: 4 to 6 servings

INGREDIENTS:

1 oz. (28g) olive oil

3 to 4 shallots (57g), or substitute 1 medium yellow onion

2 tsp. (8g) salt

3 cloves garlic, minced (about 1½ tsp. or 7g)

½ c. Unseasoned Breadcrumbs (recipe on page 135)

½ c. (50g) grated Parmesan

1½ tsp. (3g) crumbled, dried sage

2 small or 1 large butternut squash

1 whole nutmeg (or 1½ tsp. dried)

INSTRUCTIONS:

① Heat half the oil over medium heat, then reduce to medium-low. Add shallots and season with salt. Cook about 10 minutes or until soft, adding a bit of water if necessary to prevent sticking. Add garlic and cook about 5 more minutes. Sprinkle shallots around the bottom of a baking dish.

② Preheat oven to 350 degrees Fahrenheit (175 degrees Celsius). Combine breadcrumbs, cheese, and sage, and set aside. Peel, then slice the squash into ¼-inch-thick pieces. Cut out and discard seedy membrane. Toss squash slices in remaining oil, then layer them over shallots. Season with salt and a light dusting of freshly grated nutmeg. Sprinkle breadcrumb mixture over the top.

③ Cover and bake for 1 to 1½ hours or until squash is fully tender. Let pan rest about 10 minutes, then broil uncovered to brown the top. (If you can't resist, you can sprinkle on more cheese.)

PISTACHIO AND WHITE CHOCOLATE BREAD PUDDING

Bread pudding may be the best and most glorious example of worn-out, neglected, crusty old bread metamorphosing into something new and truly wonderful. As moisture is driven out of bread and starches are hardened and realigned in a process known as retrogradation, an incredibly strong structure is created. This new structure becomes a perfect home for thick, creamy custard.

Most kinds of not-too-seasoned breads are fine for use in this classic Southern dessert, but crusty breads hold up better than sandwich slices. (Save sandwich bread for turning into breadcrumbs.) If you're ready to make bread pudding but the bread is not ready for you, your refrigerator is the best place to age it (exactly why you should never store fresh bread in the refrigerator). Baked bread puddings freeze well if wrapped tightly.

If you don't happen to love pistachios and white chocolate, substitute dried cherries and dark chocolate. If you don't happen to love nuts, chocolate, or fruit, this recipe is not for you.

YIELD: 8 to 10 servings

INGREDIENTS:

1 vanilla bean or 2 tsp. (8g) vanilla extract

2 c. (454g) whole milk

6 oz. (170g) shelled pistachios (about 2 c. pistachios in the shells)

4 whole, large eggs plus 2 yolks

1 c. (238g) packed brown sugar (or substitute coconut sugar or granulated sugar)

3 c. (680g) cream (or substitute half-and-half or milk)

10 c. (525g) Unseasoned Croutons (recipe on page 134)

1½ c. (255g) white chocolate chips or chunks

INSTRUCTIONS:

① Cut vanilla bean in half lengthwise. Use back of knife to scrape all the seed paste out of the pod. Add paste and bean to heavy-bottomed saucepan with tall sides. Add milk and pistachios. Heat milk over medium-low until bubbles form around the edges (about 180 degrees Fahrenheit or 80 degrees Celsius). Remove from heat immediately. Let stand to infuse flavors.

② In a stand mixer fitted with whisk or in a blender or with a hand mixer, beat eggs on low speed until slightly thickened and lightened in color. The goal is to denature the proteins so they'll readily combine with milk to make custard.

Continued

③ Increase speed by one setting and begin adding sugar a little bit at a time, until all of it is blended. Slowly pour in cream, then turn off mixer.

④ Strain vanilla bean and pistachios out of milk. (Set vanilla bean aside to dry. Later you can add it to your sugar canister to infuse the sugar.) Set nuts aside. Slowly beat milk into egg-cream mixture.

⑤ Toss croutons, pistachios, and white chocolate pieces in a 9-by-13-inch baking pan. You can use other size pans, but may need to adjust baking time depending on depth. Pour custard over bread. Press cubes of bread down to make sure all are moistened. Cover and set aside to absorb moisture and flavor for a couple of hours, or refrigerate overnight.

⑥ Bake uncovered at 325 degrees Fahrenheit (160 degrees Celsius) for an hour or until slightly brown on top. If you like to be precise, the internal temperature should be about 165 degrees Fahrenheit (75 degrees Celsius). It's a good idea to check on it about 15 minutes before you expect it to be done. When top is slightly browned, turn broiler on for 3 to 5 minutes, keeping oven door slightly ajar. Remove when top is lightly crunchy and golden brown.

⑦ Serve warm. Pass the Bourbon and Butter Crème Anglaise so everyone can drizzle their own.

BOURBON AND BUTTER CRÈME ANGLAISE

This recipe—a favorite in our house—is about one thing: gilding the lily. Bread pudding is wonderful without any drizzle. Classic crème anglaise sauce is decadent already, and adding bourbon, butter, and brown sugar makes it crazy-amazing. Pouring this on custardy bread pudding is a wonderful way to (occasionally) celebrate all the whole-grain breads you've worked so hard to bake.

YIELD: About 2½ cups (567 grams)

INGREDIENTS:

1 vanilla bean or 2 tsp. (8g) vanilla extract

1 oz. (28g) bourbon

¼ stick (2 tbsp. or 28g) unsalted butter

1 tbsp. (14g) brown sugar

Pinch salt

½ c. (100g) granulated sugar

4 egg yolks (80g)

1¾ c. (397g) whole milk

INSTRUCTIONS:

① Cut vanilla bean in half lengthwise. Use back of knife to scrape all the seed paste out of the pod and into a small saucepan. Stir bourbon, butter, brown sugar, salt, vanilla bean, and paste together over low heat until simmering. Remove from heat to infuse while you make crème anglaise.

② In a stand mixer fitted with whisk or with a hand mixer, gradually beat ½ cup granulated sugar into egg yolks for 2 to 3 minutes, until mixture is pale yellow and forms a ribbon. (When a bit is lifted by the whip, it will fall back forming a slowly dissolving ribbon on the surface.)

③ In a heavy-bottomed saucepan, heat milk to just boiling, then gradually pour it into yolk mixture in a thin stream while continuing to beat it.

④ Pour mixture back into saucepan. Heat over medium heat while stirring continuously with a wooden spoon, until sauce thickens just enough to coat back of spoon with a light, creamy layer. Do not let custard come anywhere near a simmer (not hotter than 165 degrees Fahrenheit, or 75 degrees Celsius).

⑤ Beat sauce off heat for a minute or two to cool it. Strain through a fine sieve.

⑥ Strain vanilla bean out of infused bourbon mixture.

⑦ Whisk bourbon mixture into crème anglaise. Any leftover sauce can be gently warmed to serve on fresh fruit, ice cream, pancakes, and what-have-you over the next few days.

CRISPY COCONUT FRENCH TOAST

The open crumb of baguettes, sourdough, and no-knead breads is perfect for accepting the goodness of eggs and milk. Regular cow's milk and almond milk make great French toast, and can be used here. If you like the flavor of coconut, however, you'll die for these. The nutty flavors in many whole grains are an excellent complement to naturally sweet coconut.

This recipe requires no sugar. For a completely no-sugar-added breakfast, serve with warm almond butter and bananas instead of maple syrup.

YIELD: 4 pieces of French toast

INGREDIENTS:

4 large eggs (200g)

½ c. (113g) coconut milk (or almond or cow's milk)

2 tsp. (4g) ground cinnamon

½ tsp. (2g) salt

1 tbsp. (12g) vanilla extract

4 slices days-old bread, such as baguette, sourdough, or neutral-flavored boule

½ c. (57g) shredded, unsweetened coconut

½ stick (4 tbsp./57g) unsalted butter or substitute oil

¼ c. (65g) almond butter, warmed, for serving (optional)

1 banana, sliced, for serving (optional)

INSTRUCTIONS:

① Whisk together eggs, milk, cinnamon, salt, and vanilla. Pour into rectangular baking dish. Place bread slices in pan, flip, and press to help them soak. Depending on how stale the bread is, they may need to soak for several minutes, but rescue them before they fall apart, allowing excess to drain off.

② Scatter shredded coconut on a dry plate. Press each piece of bread firmly into shredded coconut on both sides.

③ Heat griddle to medium-high. Swirl in a pat of butter, then cook bread until golden-brown with crispy coconut. If making a large batch, keep toast in oven or toaster oven to warm.

④ Serve with optional sliced bananas, almond butter, or maple syrup.

Chapter 9

FINDING TIME TO BAKE

I don't know anyone who has more free time than they would like, yet we all end up finding time for the things we want to do most. For those who are passionate about cooking as a hobby, I don't need to help you figure out how to make time for it. However, if one of your personal goals is to do more cooking—and specifically to make healthy whole-grain foods—and you're just not sure how to fit it into an already full schedule, a few time management tricks can make it more feasible.

Many people find that the best way to squeeze baking into a busy week is to become a weekend baker. This works well because many baked goods store or freeze well or even stay fresh enough to eat for several days. Throughout the book, I have noted these things, and I've corralled some of them here again for the benefit of all you busy folks.

STORE IT

Most baked goods last well for a few days, and some for up to a week. Moist cookies, muffins, and quick breads are especially good keepers. A fruit pie might only be nice for a few days, but a loaf of sourdough bread could last a week. Most of the breads in this book are excellent keepers, because the organic acids that develop in slowly fermented breads act as natural preservatives.

The best way to store freshly baked items is to let them cool fully first. Then wrap either in a linen towel with any cut sides facing down (my favorite way), in a permeable paper bag (the traditional bakery way), or in a plastic bag (the method recommended by many baking experts). Keep at room temperature. Cooked loaves of bread also freeze well if wrapped tightly.

The worst way to store baked goods is in the refrigerator. The process by which breads lose moisture, technically known as retrogradation, accelerates between 25 and 50 degrees.

Never store bread in the refrigerator. That's the fastest way to stale it.

FREEZE IT

The following baked goods store well for several months if kept airtight in your freezer:

- Fully cooked biscuits, cookies, muffins, scones
- Shaped biscuit and scone dough, either formed into a large disc to be cut later, or precut into individual portions
- Cookie dough, in individual balls or rolled into logs that can later be sliced
- Uncooked pie crusts, rolled out and pressed into a pie pan or formed into a 4-inch disc about ¾ inch thick to be rolled out later
- Par-baked or fully baked pie crusts
- Fully baked loaves of bread
- Fully baked rolls and buns

It's up to you whether your airtight freezer container is plastic wrap, aluminum foil, a combination of both, or glass or plastic containers with lids. Here's a handy tip from King Arthur Flour's *Whole Grain Baking* book: if using flexible containers, such as zip-top bags, insert a drinking straw into the bag, seal the bag all the way to the straw, and suck out as much air as you can before sealing.

To freeze individual portions of cookie, biscuit, and scone dough so they can be cooked later, prepare their recipes to the point that the items are placed on a baking sheet. Cover

Tightly wrapped breads and baked goods are excellent freezer keepers.

the pan with plastic wrap and freeze it overnight. In the morning, pop firm, frozen biscuits, cookies, and scones into a freezer container labeled with cooking time and temperature. Don't forget the labeling part—you won't remember the directions later, and you may not recognize what the item is. When it's time to bake, don't worry about thawing. Just thaw the items as long as it takes your oven to preheat, and add a few minutes to the baking time.

REVIVE IT

To revive frozen and staling breads, first thaw them completely at room temperature. Preheat oven or toaster oven to 350 degrees Fahrenheit (177 degrees Celsius) with a baking stone in the oven if you have one. Place the bread, roll, biscuit, or what-have-you directly on the preheated stone or on a baking sheet or piece of foil, and bake 5 to 10 minutes. Larger items, such as whole loaves, take longer to refresh than small items like rolls. You might be amazed how much a stale hunk of bread can come back to life this way. Beware, however, that the heating process that refreshes bread so effectively also makes the bread even staler later. So when refreshing baked goods in a hot oven, select or cut off only the amount you want to eat right away.

MAKE IT AHEAD

One of the keys to efficient cooking is to consider recipes carefully ahead of time. Good recipes tell you what parts, if any, can be made ahead and how far ahead of time. Spending just a little time reading recipes and planning what you'll cook for the week can save you time later.

One of the best things about the timing of whole-grain baking is that you can make many doughs and batters ahead of time and let them rest. It's not only a time-saver for you, but also one of the secrets to eliciting ideal flavors and textures from whole grains.

Keeping healthy pantry staples organized and accessible is the best way to ensure that you'll actually use them.

ORGANIZE IT

Keeping the pantry and freezer stocked and well-organized is another great time-saver. I keep whole-grain flours in labeled glass jars or airtight plastic containers in my freezer. I put small quantities of flours, grains, and nuts that are leftover from recipes into a mixed-use freezer bin that I dip into frequently. I store whole, unmilled grains on a pantry shelf in glass jars and airtight 5.5-quart OXO POP containers that have been labeled with my trusty-dusty label maker (Brother P-Touch, $30, brother-usa.com). I have chosen to arrange these containers on my baking shelf in order of frequent use, but by all means, feel free to geek out with another system that works for you. The point is making it quick and easy to get to the items you need for any given cooking project.

To that end, it is also extremely helpful to have a grain mill positioned somewhere you can actually use it if you are planning to mill your own flour. Our dedicated baking

shelf houses a grain mill, a digital scale, a proofing box, a food processor (for sifting), and a few other useful odds and ends.

Our butcher block counter has twelve narrow drawers under it. Two of them are dedicated to baking tools, such as measuring cups and spoons, bowl scrapers, dough cutters, biscuit cutters, a thermometer, etc. The other ten drawers are similarly partitioned for specific uses that are important to us. Tim has two for his barbecue projects, we have one drawer for cheese-related items, and one that contains all of our most ridiculous gizmos. We call it the "James Bond drawer." We are dorks and are glad to have found one another, but that's beside the point. The point is to organize your kitchen and pantry in ways that will set you up for cooking success. Abandon traditional ideas about where things should go, and do what works for you and your household.

Why buy croutons and breadcrumbs when they're a cinch to make from stale bread? Find recipes on pages 134 and 135 .

REUSE IT

You'd be amazed how many ways leftover bread can be recharged. Find several ideas in Chapter 8.

MAKE IT WORK

The most time-consuming baking projects are yeast breads. Most of the time is hands-off if you follow the techniques outlined in this book, but you still have to plan for the total time. Refer to page 101 for specific baking plans to fit every kind of would-be baker, from those who want an occasional rustic loaf to those who aim to make their family's daily bread.

PREP IT

Finally, a word about a beautiful thing called *mise en place*. This is the French term for "putting in place." It means you begin each cooking project by setting up a work space that contains everything you'll need, and then scaling, or measuring, all your ingredients. (Note: Your work space might include the refrigerator and freezer, and mise en place might begin the night before baking.) Personally, I also include in this prep task making sure the kitchen is clean and that I have read any recipes through at least once, usually twice.

This little bit of prep work sounds so simple, but it makes a world of difference. It can mean that no ingredient accidentally gets omitted, that your measurements are correct, and that nothing scorches while you're away from the stove looking for something else.

Most importantly, mise en place means you'll have time to think while you are cooking, rather than run around finding equipment and measuring ingredients. I guess this concept has always been important to me, but when I read about it in Michael Ruhlman's book *Ruhlman's Twenty*, I dedicated myself to always thinking about why I'm doing what I'm doing whenever I cook *anything*—from now on. Why am I adding this ingredient at all, and why now? And why is it important that it be cold? How will this technique change the end result? Why am I handling this particular dough in this manner? What would happen if I turned the heat up or down? When I don't know the answers, I look them up. And I learn. And I'm a better cook next time.

Do the same—prep, and then think—and I guarantee you will have more kitchen successes than failures.

EPILOGUE

A few years ago, I had an interesting conversation with my boss, Bryan Welch, publisher of *Mother Earth News*, *Mother Earth Living*, and a number of other magazines with a food focus. I was toying with the idea of writing a book about making homemade versions of foods we all normally buy—such as flour—and we ended up bemoaning the fact that most cookbooks and food magazines focus on recipes and occasionally, thank goodness, techniques. What they tend not to focus on is the nature of ingredients—where they come from, who produced them, and how. "No one seems to care about the provenance of the ingredients," he said. "I'd like to see that cookbook."

Lucky for all of us, times have changed somewhat since that conversation, and mine is neither the first nor the only book to focus on quality ingredients. Still, I find the discussion of food sourcing to be generally lacking in cookbooks and food magazines. A recipe is not enough. *What* you put in the bowl matters even more than *how much*.

Visit www.bourbonandbutter.com for much more detailed ingredient and equipment information, including recommended suppliers of whole-grain flours, unmilled whole grains, and other high-quality real food ingredients; recommended manufacturers of durable, well-made kitchen equipment, including all types of grain mills; handy whole grain measurement guides; favorite cookbooks, cooking tips, and resources; plus more recipes and inspiration.

I hope wherever you live, you are spoiled rotten with ingredients of enviable provenance. I hope you are lucky enough to know the names of the farmers who grow your food, and I hope they grow especially flavorful and nutritious food in conscientious ways.

I live down the street from a farmers market where I can buy freshly ground flour, of heirloom variety even. A few blocks further is a natural foods co-op stocking bulk grains, milled and unmilled. A couple of towns over, there's a century-old grain mill where you can buy flour today. Still, I often turn to online sources and national brands in my quest for quality. If you get serious about cooking with a variety of real ingredients, you probably will too.

A detailed discussion of all potential baking ingredients is beyond the scope of this book, but I would be remiss if I failed to put in a plug for choosing the healthiest and most sustainable versions of animal products. Butter, milk and cream, yogurt, eggs, lard, and meat from animals raised humanely and sustainably are superior to commercial, industrial food (the stuff in most grocery stores) in nearly every way possible. Besides being nutritionally superior, these ingredients often have better baking qualities, too. If you've ever cracked open a fresh egg from pastured chickens or made a pie crust with real lard, you know what I'm talking about. To learn more about the scientifically proven benefits of sustainably raised animal products, visit www.eatwild.com.

ACKNOWLEDGMENTS

The sun was setting outside the Tap Room in Lawrence, Kansas. Tim Nauman (this book's photographer) and I were two or three Clontarfs in. The plan to craft a cookbook about down-and-dirty DIY cooking was hatched. It was our first date. Four years and one rad specimen of offspring later, here I sit in awe of the fact that the first of our many mutual aspirations has come to fruition; that more than occasionally, our crazy shared dreams are realized; that Tim and I are doing work together every day that we love, love, love. Thank you, Tim, for standing at the sink, the stove, the counter, the bar . . . right by my side.

It was nuts for us to take on a cookbook project during our first year of parenting. We have many friends and family who know this to be true. The actual business of going to work each day would have been unthinkable without the practical support of our families, especially our moms. Sonja, you are a master of props acquisition and baby distraction. Also, there is a good chance I wouldn't be doing what I do today were it not for numerous childhood practice sessions. Carol, you will always rule Mondays. Reading book after book on the porch swing with Jupiter gave us much needed photo-shoot time.

Friends, too, have much to do with this work's genesis and completion: the bottomless well of love and loyalty that is VPC; the wordly inspiration of Miss Jenny Noble Anderson; the tremendous emotional support of Yoga Bellies, our parenting tribe; the Jupiter love showered on us by Brandy Alterman, Heather Scott, Ali Calkins, Rose Naughtin, and Sommer Brechiesen, among other awesome babysitting friends; and the lovely ladies and gents holding down the fort for us in NYC. And actually, New York, I owe you a debt of gratitude, too. Good God, your food is as good as your energy is endless. I've eaten so well. I've learned so much. I'm still in love. Thanks also to all of you who helped test recipes to make sure instructions were clear and flavors memorable.

Obviously, I did not bake the first loaf of bread. Everyone who is lucky enough to make their livelihood by trading in food or words owes something to someone. I have many culinary heroes. Read about them on my website, bourbonandbutter.com.

Professionally, I want to thank my biggest supporters at Ogden Publications. Cheryl Long, you've been as much a friend as a mentor. Bryan Welch, because of you, I begin every writing assignment with sights set on surprise and delight. Jennifer Kongs and Shelley Stonebrook, your enthusiasm is like a rechargeable battery that keeps me keepin' on. K. C. Compton, you're one of my favorite cheerleaders. I hope to have a relationship with words as rich, fun, and funny as yours someday. Jessica Kellner, you make my job easy and enjoyable. I appreciate your flexibility and the generous accommodation of my baby-having and cookbook-writing schedules. For the wisdom and consultation on my road to becoming a person who writes books, thank you, Barbara Pleasant. William Woys Weaver, oh how I have enjoyed working with you over the years. I'm humbled that you found this project worthy of your input.

I have many folks to thank for the putting together of these pages. Megan E. Phelps, you've been my comrade for so many years. For the after-work beers at The Pig, the gifts of foraged mushrooms and homegrown tomatoes, and especially the hours and hours you spent reading this manuscript and making it better, I owe you so much. Elizabeth Noll, you paid me the most generous compliment of my professional life by asking me to write this book. Thank you to the many folks at Voyageur/Quarto who took the torch from Elizabeth and got this book made: Madeleine Vasaly, Brittany Stojsavljevic, Cindy Laun, Carol Holtz, and Diana Boger. To Katie Fawkes and her marketing team, we are just beginning our work together. I have much to learn, and I'm looking forward to it. Kim Wallace, I'm looking at you too, friend. You always inspire me to get the word out about things that matter.

Finally, Heidi Alterman, my dear sister, we've created and destroyed many a Best Sugar Cookie together. I doubt I'd be doing what I do today without those precious times.

PHOTOGRAPHER'S NOTES

I like grains. I like the basic grains I was fed as a child and the ones that are readily available at any store. I don't like most foods that are "good for you." Why? Because most of the time, they don't taste good.

I was honored to be asked to take the photographs for this book. I love food, and I love making things look beautiful. At the topic, I groaned a bit. As the author's partner, I'd surely have to taste a bunch of healthy stuff. As we began to have our photo styling meetings, I steeled myself for an onslaught of dense nutrition.

I was wrong. Happily wrong. I didn't know what decadence would arrive in the form of Almond-Berry Dark Chocolate Cake (page 114), what savory goodness would be found in Shrimp-and-Grit Muffins (page 36), that I already loved Tabitha's Multigrain Waffles (page 39)—not realizing how healthy they'd always been. And the bread! Eat the Basic Sourdough (page 91) immediately—well, you'll have to wait for a bit, but it's worth it.

Could it be that these foods were not only nutritionally better than their white counterparts, but they actually tasted great? To Rye Coconut Banana Bread (page 34) and Buckwheat Crêpes (page 41), Whole-Wheat Pie Crust (page 51) and Sourdough Hamburger Buns (page 94), I have been converted. Because these are better than anything I can buy. As work on this book progressed, so did the rhythm of baking in our house. Quickly and somehow easily, I became something of a baker too.

I hope you enjoy the images in this book, have fun making the recipes, and, most of all, experience the satisfaction that results from making great food.

—Tim Nauman

RECOMMENDED RESOURCES

WHOLE GRAINS AND WHOLE-GRAIN FLOURS

Most of these companies offer organic and non-GMO unmilled whole grains and flours, plus a wide range of baking ingredients. Some of these retailers supply natural and mainstream grocery stores nationwide, as well.

Alter Eco www.altereco-usa.com

Ancient Harvest www.ancientharvest.com

Anson Mills www.ansonmills.com

Arrowhead Mills www.arrowheadmills.com

Bluebird Grain Farms www.bluebirdgrainfarms.com

Bob's Red Mill www.bobsredmill.com

Daisy Organic Flour www.daisyflour.com

Dakota Prairie Organic Flour Co. www.dakota-prairie.com

Eden Foods www.edenfoods.com

Full Belly Farm www.fullbellyfarm.com

Great River Organic Milling www.greatrivermilling.com

Heartland Mill www.heartlandmill.com

Hodgson Mill www.hodgsonmill.com

Jovial Foods www.jovialfoods.com

King Arthur Flour www.kingarthurflour.com

Lehman's www.lehmans.com

Lotus Foods www.lotusfoods.com

Lundberg Family Farms www.lundberg.com

Montana Milling www.montanamilling.com

Pleasant Hill Grain www.pleasanthillgrain.com

Shiloh Farms www.shilohfarms.com

Sunrise Flour Mill www.sunriseflourmill.com

Sun Organic Farm www.sunorganic.com

To Your Health Sprouted Flour Co.
www.organicsproutedflour.net

The Urban Homemaker www.urbanhomemaker.com

Wheat Montana Farms www.wheatmontana.com

Wild Hive Farm www.wildhivefarm.com

THE WHOLE GRAIN LOVER'S LIBRARY

Breads

Amy's Bread by Amy Scherber and Toy Kim Dupree

The Art of Baking with Natural Yeast by Caleb Warnock and Melissa Richardson

Bread: A Baker's Book of Techniques and Recipes by Jeffrey Hamelman

Bread: A Global History by William Rubel

The Bread Baker's Apprentice: Mastering the Art of Extraordinary Bread by Peter Reinhart

Bread Making: Crafting the Perfect Loaf from Crust to Crumb by Lauren Chattman

Beard on Bread by James Beard

Classic Sourdoughs, Revised: A Home Baker's Handbook by Ed Wood and Jean Wood

Healthy Bread in Five Minutes a Day: 100 New Recipes Featuring Whole Grains, Fruits, Vegetables, and Gluten-Free Ingredients by Jeff Hertzberg and Zoë François

King Arthur Flour Whole Grain Baking: Delicious Recipes Using Nutritious Whole Grains by P. J. Hamel, Susan Reid, and Susan Miller

The Laurel's Kitchen Bread Book by Laurel Robertson

Local Breads: Sourdough and Whole-Grain Recipes from Europe's Best Artisan Bakers by Daniel Leader

My Bread by Jim Lahey

The New Artisan Bread in Five Minutes a Day: The Discovery That Revolutionizes Home Baking by Jeff Hertzberg and Zoë François

No Need to Knead by Suzanne Dunaway

Simply Great Breads: Sweet and Savory Yeasted Treats from America's Premier Artisan Baker by Daniel Leader

Tartine Bread by Chad Robertson

Tartine Book No. 3: Modern Ancient Classic Whole by Chad Robertson

Whole Grain Breads by Peter Reinhart

Whole Grains

Ancient Grains for Modern Meals: Mediterranean Whole Grain Recipes for Barley, Farro, Kamut, Polenta, Wheat Berries, and More by Maria Speck

Good to the Grain: Baking with Whole-Grain Flours by Kim Boyce

The Homemade Flour Cookbook: The Home Cook's Guide to Milling Nutritious Flours and Creating Delicious Recipes with Every Grain, Legume, Nut, and Seed from A–Z by Erin Alderson

The New Book of Whole Grains: More Than 200 Recipes Featuring Whole Grains by Marlene A. Bumgarner

The New Whole Grain Cookbook: Terrific Recipes Using Farro, Quinoa, Brown Rice, Barley, and Many Other Delicious and Nutritious Grains by Robin Asbell

The Splendid Grain by Rebecca Wood

The Whole Grain Cookbook by A. D. Livingston

Whole-Grain Mornings: New Breakfast Recipes to Span the Seasons by Megan Gordon

Whole Grains Every Day, Every Way by Lorna Sass

Baking Science and Techniques

Bakewise: The Hows and Whys of Successful Baking with Over 200 Magnificent Recipes by Shirley O. Corriher

Bread Science: The Chemistry and Craft of Making Bread by Emily Buehler

I'm Just Here for More Food: Food x Mixing + Heat = Baking by Alton Brown

Mastering the Art of French Cooking by Julia Child, Louisette Bertholle, Simone Beck, and Sidonie Coryn

On Food and Cooking: The Science and Lore of the Kitchen by Harold McGee

Ratio: The Simple Codes Behind the Craft of Everyday Cooking by Michael Ruhlman

Ruhlman's Twenty: 20 Techniques 100 Recipes A Cook's Manifesto by Michael Ruhlman

INDEX

ABOUT the AUTHOR

Personally and professionally, Tabitha Alterman has always felt at home working with food or words, and she has aligned those passions at every opportunity. Over the past fifteen years, these interests have taken her from a small restaurant in Memphis, Tennessee, to an organic coffee farm in Hawai'i to a community garden and a United Nations delegate position in New York City. Tabitha is currently growing a small garden and a small family in Lawrence, Kansas, where she develops recipes, writes about food, and cooks and styles food for photo shoots. She is the Food and Garden editor for *Mother Earth Living* magazine and contributing editor for *Mother Earth News*, the nation's leading sustainable lifestyles publications. Visit her website at bourbonandbutter.com.